D0762871

The Prodigal Brother

Making Peace with Your Parents, Your Past, and the Wayward One in Your Family

SUE THOMPSON

WestBow
PRESS

Copyright © 2010 Susan J. Thompson

All rights reserved. No part of this book may be used or reproduced by any means, graphic, electronic, or mechanical, including photocopying, recording, taping or by any information storage retrieval system without the written permission of the publisher except in the case of brief quotations embodied in critical articles and reviews.

WestBow Press books may be ordered through booksellers or by contacting:

WestBow Press
A Division of Thomas Nelson
1663 Liberty Drive
Bloomington, IN 47403
www.westbowpress.com
1-(866) 928-1240

Because of the dynamic nature of the Internet, any Web addresses or links contained in this book may have changed since publication and may no longer be valid. The views expressed in this work are solely those of the author and do not necessarily reflect the views of the publisher, and the publisher hereby disclaims any responsibility for them.

ISBN: 978-1-4497-0053-9 (sc)
ISBN: 978-1-4497-0054-6 (hc)
ISBN: 978-1-4497-0052-2 (e)

Library of Congress Control Number: 2010901378

Printed in the United States of America

WestBow Press rev. date: 04/19/2010

I am humbled by the support and devotion of my husband, the love of my life, Larry. Talk about "unmerited favor"! You are a gift.

This book is dedicated to my father, my mother, and my brother. If only I had not fought so hard against what God put in my way. He had a plan and worked it in spite of me.

"... so is my word that goes out from my mouth: It will not return to me empty, but will accomplish what I desire and achieve the purpose for which I sent it" (Isaiah 55:11).

Table of Contents

Chapter 1 We Are All Far from Home 1
Chapter 2 Born Wounded 11
Chapter 3 Journey to a Distant Land 25
Chapter 4 I Used to Be a Pharisee 39
Chapter 5 Dancing As Fast As I Can 55
Chapter 6 Sitting by the Spring of My Injustices 67
Chapter 7 First We Must Grieve 83
Chapter 8 If You Don't Love, You Don't Know 97
Chapter 9 Trust and Gratitude 113
Chapter 10 The Light Will Reveal 123
Chapter 11 My Machine of Hideous Beauty 135
Chapter 12 Climbing the Mountain of Forgiveness 147
Chapter 13 Standing on the Summit 163
Notes 177

— CHAPTER ONE —

We Are All Far From Home

There was a man who had two sons. The younger one said to his father, "Father, give me my share of the estate." So he divided his property between them. Not long after that, the younger son got together all he had, set off for a distant country and there squandered his wealth in wild living. After he had spent everything, there was a severe famine in that whole country, and he began to be in need. So he went and hired himself out to a citizen of that country, who sent him to his fields to feed the pigs. He longed to fill his stomach with the pods that the pigs were eating, but no one gave him anything.

When he came to his senses, he said, "How many of my father's hired men have food to spare, and here I am starving to death! I will set out and go back to my father and say to him: Father, I have sinned against heaven and against you. I am no longer worthy to be called your son; make me like one of your hired men." So he got up and went to his father.

But while he was still a long way off, his father saw him and was filled with compassion for him; he ran to his son, threw his arms around him and kissed him. The son said to him, "Father, I have sinned against heaven and against you. I am no longer worthy to be called your son." But the father said to his servants, "Quick! Bring the best robe and put it on him. Put a ring on his finger and sandals on his feet. Bring the fattened calf and kill it. Let's have a feast and celebrate. For this son of mine was dead and is alive again; he was lost and is found." So they began to celebrate.

Meanwhile, the older son was in the field. When he came near the house, he heard music and dancing. So he called one of the servants and asked him what was going on. "Your brother has come," he replied, "and your father has killed the fattened calf because he has him back safe and sound."

The older brother became angry and refused to go in. So his father went out and pleaded with him. But he answered his father, "Look! All these years I've been slaving for you and never disobeyed your orders. Yet you never gave me even a young goat so I could celebrate with my friends. But when this son of yours who has squandered your property with prostitutes comes home, you kill the fattened calf for him!" "My son," the father said, "you are always with me, and everything I have is yours. But we had to celebrate and be glad, because this brother of yours was dead and is alive again; he was lost and is found."

—LUKE 15:11-32

I used to travel with an evangelist who had been a cocktail waitress in Las Vegas. Whenever she told the story of her sad, drug-addicted life before she became a Christian, people were on the edge of their seats. She had a wonderful, honest sense of humor; crowds would howl with laughter over her stories about her naive attempts to talk about God with the busboys, waitresses, and blackjack dealers with whom she worked. She would end with a powerful call to those whose lives were as misused and as damaged as hers had been, urging them to come and meet the One who could make all things new.

Not everyone has a personal story like my evangelist friend, of setting off to throw away his or her life, but we thrill to hear exciting testimonies that play for us again the story of the prodigal. There's nothing we love more than to hear of a battered life given a fresh chance. It's the expression of an eternal hope: that God is so loving toward us He will enable us to open just one eye, even halfway, to see where we are and where we need to be and then give us the strength to make the walk to His mercy.

Because of this, we often make celebrities out of folks who have a captivating testimony. When I was a new believer in the 1970s, it seemed that church services and Christian radio and television programs were filled with dramatic accounts of tormented lives turned around by Jesus Christ. Those who had been raised in stable, God-fearing families and had invited Jesus into their hearts at a young age often felt, in comparison, they had nothing to share. Their histories weren't as impressive as "Born to Be Wild—Until I Met Jesus" or "How I Experienced Complete Ruin Before I Found the Lord."

It took some of us a while to realize simple testimonies of childhood conversions are as powerful and as impressive as accounts of a life wasted. When God prevents a journey of emptiness and pain, it's as much of a miraculous intervention as those other sensational reports. We've come to realize, too, that we are all prodigals, regardless of our stories. We must all come to our senses wherever we are and walk toward that cross on the hill.

There are two brothers in the parable of the prodigal son, and we usually focus our attention on the younger one. Now there's a testimony! Demanding his share of the family wealth, he ran off to another country, spent it on wild living and prostitutes, and ended up so broke he fed pigs just to get by. As all parents of prodigals pray their children will do, he came to a stinging realization of how good it had been at home, where even men his father hired to do menial work had far more than he did. "No one gave him anything," the story tells us, and in such a rotten place he longed to be treated as generously as a field worker on his father's land. The younger brother was broken by the consequences of his decisions and saw this clearly enough to head for home.

The older brother, though, who stayed home and never demanded anything of his family, holds little interest for us other than to invite our scorn: why isn't he happy that his brother came home? Why can't he rejoice with the father? Time and time again when the story is read, the older brother's reaction is used to illustrate pride, haughty superiority, ungratefulness, and much more.

A friend wrote me after I gave her my thoughts about this parable. She said, "I think the brother who stayed at home should have been slapped. He had an attitude that was less honorable than his brother who thoroughly repented, had a submitting experience, and came with honor and respect for his father. The prodigal son may have been arrogant, cavalier, lazy . . . but he knew how to repent and then submit. I am sure he became the model of what we are supposed to be after we turn from our sinful lives."

I don't disagree with my friend's visceral reaction to the response of the son who stayed behind, the one I call the "prodigal brother" because, like the prodigal son, he also had a journey to make. He is there as a shadow in the bright light of the ultimate point of the story. His pained behavior provides a contrast to the deep compassion the father has for the son who has returned home.

But parables can have many dimensions of meaning. We can view them from the front and see what appears to be all there is, but as we walk around the story and stand at the side or in the back we see details that were not visible to us at first. There was an immediate context to the relationships Jesus was describing in the parable of the lost son. No one who heard Jesus tell the story missed that God was calling to the sons who had left the family, and light was being focused on the conceited attitude of the Pharisees. They were the "older brothers" who had stayed within the fold and who claimed the inheritance of Abraham and Moses, but whose hearts were blind to God's desires and intentions. Jesus described their vanity in the parable of the Pharisee who stood apart from the tax collector in the temple and proclaimed in prayer, "God, I thank you that I am not like other men . . . even like this tax collector" (Luke 18:11). Their pride is evidenced in the older brother's refusal to enter the house where the younger brother was being celebrated. The Pharisees saw themselves as truly *better* than everyone because they adhered to all the rules of a rule-making tradition. They could barely bring themselves to associate with the unclean, uninitiated masses and would avoid them, or at least openly express disapproval of their condition.

I have no problem seeing the "frontal view" of this parable. It is clear to me that Jesus wanted to show His listeners the Father desired His lost sons to return because He loved them. He also wanted the "older brothers" to understand the spirit of the Law and the Prophets and rejoice with the Father when wayward children come home. But I understand the older brother. I relate to him more than to anyone else in the story. Like many who share a similar tale, I had a sibling who gave his life over to drugs and alcohol. His impairments, his inability to thrive rightly, affected my family in the most profound ways. He was the prodigal and I was the dutiful older child who stayed at home.

My brother's story is woven into my own. I can trace deep roots of unforgiveness in my life to my attitudes regarding my family. I am aware of my natural tendency to compartmentalize my feelings and can easily track this to the need I had as a child to protect my heart from the troubles at home.

Most dismaying, I also recognize the weight of sin in my life, particularly where it springs from the well of my family's dysfunctions. My need to prove that I am worthy of recognition, that I won't degenerate into helplessness—these sins of arrogance, pride, and contempt I feel most heavily when I remember my family life.

I'm not proud of these attitudes. They are the fallout of destructive experiences, and I hate how they linger. I wish I were a far more compassionate, forgiving human being with an empathetic understanding of how difficult parenting can be. I do not have children, but I know no matter how great parents might be, children can decide to be foolish and hateful. In spite of all the good a mom and dad can provide, some kids have to learn the hard way.

We who embraced the good parenting and made good decisions may not realize our stories, though vastly different from that of the prodigal child, have the same ultimate result. We need forgiveness too! But more than the younger brother, we older brothers need help to see all that's happened and recognize our need for forgiveness. The younger son had to come to his senses; so must the older son. I tend to think our job is a bit harder. The younger brother didn't have to look very hard to see the wretchedness of his condition and throw himself at his father's mercy. We big brothers and sisters have a less obvious predicament. Our misery is not about being barefoot and hungry, but it is nevertheless a product of a particular kind of starvation.

Lots of challenges in a family can create a prodigal: substance abuse, mental illness, physical sickness, learning disorders, or any problem that forces parents to focus on one child more than another. It could be the unfortunate weakness of parents who are simply incapable of making the painful decisions necessary for the family's well-being. Sometimes parents just don't know what to do, even though we think they should. We cling to an illusion that our parents ought to have been prepared for what assailed them and our childhood judgments can smolder in the ashes of their failures. If I have any insight, if I have any light to shed upon the deeper issues of growing up among the agonizing problems of a family affected by a child who is an alcoholic or drug addict, I share them out of the knowledge that I am not alone. We need help to find our way to the Father's door. I can tell you of my own travel home, and maybe it will help you.

To be sure, Jesus' account of these two brothers and their father does not mirror my family circumstances point by point, for my brother never came home with repentance and humility. In this particular tale, I see myself in the older brother, a Pharisee, an embittered child, even if all of the other parts of the story don't quite fit. I can hear the words of the Master to me in a powerful way through this parable.

Let's look at the two brothers. We know about the journey of the lost son, who came to his senses and made the decision to return to his father and plead for nothing more than a place among the family servants. His journey home began the moment he realized he had depleted the resources he'd been given and his stomach cried out to be filled with pigs' food. He packed whatever little he had left and set out to return to his father's house. Remember, he was in a "distant country." He had to find his way home, a journey that might take many days, perhaps weeks or months. As he sought a ride with a caravan or walked alone through the famine-ravaged land, he must have had a lot of time to think about what he had done, what it said about his character, what reception he might face. I can imagine that with each day he traveled, he became more and more aware of how foolish he had been and maybe a little frightened he would experience the rejection his culture expected.

The older brother also had a journey to make, a journey of the heart, where he saw the relationship for which he longed but had become too hardened to receive. The older son stayed physically close by while he moved emotionally farther and farther away from intimate connection with his father. He seethed with angry judgment, allowing it to overtake him. Jesus does not tell us anything about the family or how personalities played out. Because we usually see only the direct view of the parable, we don't naturally assume the father, representing God, had anything to do with the older son's refusal to join the celebration of his brother's return. But if we read it as the story of a family, if we read it while standing in the field with the older brother, we can identify the reasons for the frustration shown at the father's jubilation. We who are prodigal brothers—the good kids who stayed behind—can explain without hesitation why we prefer to be out in the field rather than inside the house, where there seems to be nothing but constant mourning over the younger brother's absence and, as is often the case, little to no acknowledgment our presence is valued for its own sake.

For many reasons, we prodigal brothers could not rejoice with our parents when the younger son returned because we knew what would happen. Our joy was tapped out after years of watching our brother or sister come home with a sob story designed to elicit relief. We watched with dismay as our parents, filled with a desperate love we could not understand, gave their all, believing it would make a difference. Today we see our conclusions about them gave us fuel to keep the fires of resentment burning.

What is our payoff, prodigal brothers, for fanning our flames of hurt and bitterness? We, too, have to set down the pail in our hands and come to our senses. We can never go back and change the past. What we *can* do is change the direction in which we are heading. We can stop just long enough to see we're stuck in the middle of a field we created with our pain. We can decide to enter our Father's house.

"Home," wrote Henri Nouwen, "is the center of my being where I can hear the voice that says, 'You are my Beloved, on you my favor rests'—the same voice that gave life to the first Adam and spoke to Jesus, the second Adam; the same voice that speaks to all the children of God and sets them free to live in the midst of a dark world while remaining in the light."[1]

Whether a person squanders a life in wild living or in smoldering resentment, he or she is far from home. Failure to let go of past hurts can exhaust us in ways we do not recognize. The Father has come to plead with us to lay down our heartache and resentment. He calls us to release the bitterness and judgment we've carried for so long and join in the festivities that belong to us, too. The house is so close we can hear the party from where we stand, toiling away, hoping to be noticed. Let's walk to it. Father is there.

— Chapter Two —

Born Wounded

Is there a way out? I don't think there is—at least not on my side. It often seems that the more I try to disentangle myself from the darkness, the darker it becomes. I need light, but that light has to conquer my darkness, and that I cannot bring about by myself. I cannot forgive myself. I cannot make myself feel loved. By myself I cannot leave the land of my anger. I cannot bring myself home nor can I create communion on my own. I can desire it, hope for it, wait for it, yes, pray for it. But my true freedom I cannot fabricate for myself. That must be given to me. I am lost. I must be found and brought home by the shepherd who goes out to me.

—HENRI NOUWEN[1]

He was as cute as they come. The closest my little lips could get to "brother" was "burder," and in home movies I see that darling burder of mine, a smile on his face, as he stares into the camera on a winter afternoon in Coonskin Park. I watch my young self grab him and plant a kiss on him, and we both look at my father as he films the scene, our faces beaming.

I had been adopted just a few years before. Mom and Dad had been married for 8 years when Dad's coworker in a West Virginia finance office mentioned she was caring for a baby who had been left with her and her mother. The woman's friend had delivered out of wedlock and asked for help in finding a family who wanted a child. When my father heard about it, he arranged to go and take a look at the abandoned infant. "I peered over the top of that bassinette and you grinned up at me and shook that leg," he would tell me over and over again throughout the years, each time with a big smile. "It was all over for me right then." Mom had miscarried in the past and was worried she might not be able to carry a child to term. She would say, "The moment I took you in my arms, I could not let you go."

Just a few months after I became their child, my parents were thrilled by the news my mother was pregnant. Doctors kept a close watch on her progress and, as had happened before, she began bleeding. This time, however, physicians rushed her into the hospital for a Cesarean and were able to save the tiny baby, two months premature. My father would tell us he was so small his legs were "no bigger around than my pinky finger."

My brother survived in a day when neonatal care seems almost primitive compared to today's medical advancements. But something occurred in that birth and during his time in the hospital that imprinted upon my little brother something irreversible. We know much more today about children's emotional development than we did in 1957, and it helps me understand my brother to know he was in an incubator and separated from my mother for weeks after he was surgically removed from her womb. Today, a mother would be encouraged to touch the baby and hold it if at all possible, because the mother's touch is required for a healthy bonding, for the laying of that internal foundation of being wanted and loved. But not many in the medical community understood that then, and babies in neonatal units didn't have the same kind of contact with their parents that is common today. Where mother and father are now routinely encouraged to be at the child's side as much as possible, even around the clock, back then it was "visiting hours only." The physical touch incubator babies received came most often from the nurses and doctors attending them, and this is not the touch a baby instinctively craves. It deeply needs to connect with its mother from birth, by touch, by breastfeeding, by her cooing and talking and kissing, by falling asleep in its mother's arms.

When a baby doesn't receive this within the first few days or weeks after birth, a powerful defense can be called into action: infants interpret the separation as abandonment and turn inward. If no one is there for long periods of time, the baby simply stops searching and folds up that tiny heart, making it unavailable to anyone outside.

From the moment a little one makes that inward turn, unless there is some awareness and continued, applied effort, he or she can be closed to the love and sustenance provided. It's not impossible to unfold a heart—many children are brought back from the brink of self-protective isolation by consistent affection and attention. "No one knows how many interruptions a child's spirit can tolerate before permanent damage occurs," wrote nurse-therapist Jane Ryan in her book *Broken Spirits Lost Souls*.[2]

My mother and father were frequently allowed in past visiting hours, but had to leave my brother to the nurses' daily care until they finally took him home. My cousin lived with my parents for a while after graduating from high school and told me, "I don't remember how long it was before he came home, but it seemed like forever." If it seemed like forever to a young adult, think of how long it must have felt to an infant in a sterile environment. Once he was deemed ready to go, he was handed to my parents with the assumption he would never remember the experience; he was just a baby. Years later, my mother wondered if his being so long separated from her could have been a reason he was so broken.

There were other factors that shaped my little brother's internal foundation; his development was affected by multiple obstacles that set him on a road to destruction. Even so, from the time my parents were finally allowed to bring him home, he was difficult. He cried constantly. Nothing seemed to satisfy him. He was not comforted by their care. My brother was needy, rejecting, and demanding. He was sensitive to everything and soothed by little. The stress of his bottomless needs was enormous for many months to come.

"Keep this to show Dan when he grows up," wrote my mother a couple of years after his birth on a piece of paper where she had noted his early feeding schedule. "He had to be fed every three hours—24 hours daily. I was afraid he would not get enough to eat—that's why I recorded his intake at each feeding! . . . It sure was rough on Momma, old Danny boy! Hope you appreciate me and your dad!" This was a child they wanted and loved. This was not a baby born to parents who did not know how to cherish what they had been given. They poured themselves into him from the beginning. It's hard to view the misshapen trajectory of his life when it began with such hope and commitment.

I can imagine as my mother and father attended to my brother, they did the things that had worked with me and countless other babies. They stroked, they rocked, they patted, walking the floor and whispering to the little one he was going to be all right. But what satisfied me did nothing for him. He screamed louder, distraught and despondent. Nothing helped. As he got older and could relate his fears, he seemed unwilling to be comforted, unable to absorb their consolation. In some strange way, their tenderness and care seemed to make things worse. I think of their exhaustion and dismay and I wonder how they made it through his early years.

Just as those days closed out, new challenges arose. As he grew, anger pooled like a leak from a broken pipe, and then became a flood. My little brother could burst into rages of screaming and crying and, even in first grade, cussing like an adult. He had virtually no attention span. He was violent. He destroyed property and laughed at harming animals. No amount of punishment or disciplinary tactics reined him in. My parents' tools were limited and the one they used most was spanking with my father's belt or a thin switch from a tree. While this may elicit gasps of dismay, the fact is my parents were not abusive in their discipline and I cannot ever remember being physically harmed. I realize now it wasn't the most effective disciplinary tool; my brother simply did not respond to physical punishment. The frustration he would exhibit after being spanked was intense; he would sit, rocking hard into the back of a chair, cursing, crying, spitting, and vowing to kill my parents when he got the chance.

Danny was filled with fear. When he was little, he wouldn't taste foods he'd eaten the day before because they didn't "smell right." He feared the dark. He was afraid of sleeping in a room alone, or of having the door shut. I have youthful memories of my brother waking up in the middle of the night screaming, terrified by a recurring dream of being in a dark hole. One expects childhood fears such as looking under the bed or being in a dark place, but my brother's fears were irrational and he carried them into adulthood. For example, he feared the dentist. By the time he was in his thirties, his mouth was full of cavities and blackened teeth—he simply quit going for checkups after leaving home; he'd rather bear pain than face the dentist's chair. He feared the doctor and would go only if he could take advantage of a free clinic when he had a minor problem or was forced by the rules of a rehab facility. He feared dying to the point of sobbing when he spoke of it.

My brother survived a tremendous trauma to enter the world, and after a lengthy separation from his mother he was handed to her as though there were nothing wrong—but in fact, everything was wrong and he never recovered. Every child is born with his or her individual strengths and weaknesses. Some weaknesses are made by congenital malfunctions or impacts too significant to overcome, as in my brother's case. Another child might experience greater challenges but emerge strong and healthy. Just as with adults, the same experiences will not affect children in the same ways. Who can understand why one child is broken and another endures? I believe my brother's little spirit was simply fragile from the beginning.

Not every person who becomes a drug addict or alcoholic has a tragic birth story, but in my brother's case, I am convinced he was weakened at the earliest stage of life and had no emotional tools with which to face the world. He was learning disabled. His IQ was low and, after taking him for psychological evaluation at a local college, my parents were told he was "borderline mentally retarded," a fact they repeated often as evidence of his "limitations." I resisted this assessment. I was furious they gave in so easily to an explanation that had no meaning when it came to the way they dealt with him. Developmentally disabled or not, he was not given the tools for facing real life because my parents could not bring themselves to make hard decisions; decisions that seemed cold and uncaring, and even when they tried, they faced a barrage of ferocious behaviors. Eventually, every tantrum, every crazy incident—not just the tantrums and incidents of childhood but all through his life—was met with a quick fix and a payoff to prevent further disruption.

After the psychological testing we had an appointment or two with a family therapist. Certainly my parents must have hoped that something would change, that finding out what my brother's impairments were would make some kind of difference. But we didn't continue counseling. Years later I asked my dad about it. "It was too far to drive," he told me.

We had moved to California just before my brother's 7th birthday. Not too long after that he was brought home by the police, caught attempting to break into a pay phone. He was taking drugs by the end of the 1960s, before he was 12. He dropped out of school at 15 and lived a life characterized by bad relationships, months away from home, and drunk-driving arrests.

Danny was completely without self-control. When angered he could scream and swear and fight as though his very life depended upon it, and he knew he could coerce my parents into just about anything. I try to remember good things about him, but after a certain age there is nothing but the memory of cruel and hateful behavior, of a life of dissipation. He was extreme in everything. His language was shockingly foul, his friends witless and gross, his hygiene indifferent. I remember my parents yelling and pleading and arguing with him, and I watched him win every time. Even when they seemed to win, they lost, because while their intentions remained steadfast, they just couldn't seem to follow through on their commitments to discipline.

For a while, around the time he was 20 years old, my parents wrote their prayers in a small brown binder. Page follows page in which they wrote out heartfelt pleas for his protection, his salvation, his relationships. "You are aware of the attempted attack on Danny's life last week . . . take him completely out of these gangland-type attacks and the fear accompanying them." "Give him a job . . ." "Prosper him financially, cause him to want a clean and sanitary home for himself . . ." "Today he told us that he and his girlfriend were married in Mexico . . ." And finally, "We are confident in Your performing all of these things in his life from this night forward. We thank You and trust You completely in Jesus' name." After some of the prayers, my mother noted, "Not answered." I read these prayers with sadness. My parents could not see that when they gave in to their desperate impulses to help him, they were not helping him, and they saw these failures as unanswered prayers. They could not see the situation honestly.

Jane Ryan calls kids like my brother "impression managers." She writes, "Most attachment compromised youngsters seem to have an inborn sense of how, and who, to 'work' so their needs will be met."[3] Danny could put on a face of angelic contrition. He could plead with a flattery and charm that sucked them in. When that didn't work, he ramped up his responses for shock value: he cursed. He screamed. He verbally abused our parents as they sat in their chairs in the den. He threw things, slammed furniture into walls, told them he was going to put them in wheelchairs. I wanted to grab him and push him right out the front door, throw his clothes after him, and tell him to get lost, but not my parents. My father would sit, quietly suffering, while my mother cried out, "Why do you hate us? Why do you act like this?" He'd stomp out of the house, calling over his shoulder that they were worthless and he hoped they would die soon. Later, they'd sit him down, pull out the wallet, and hand over what he had demanded—but of course, only after giving him a stern reprimand they thought had some significance.

My parents dealt with my brother out of tremendous guilt and self-recrimination. When Danny was young it was believed that everything we become was the sole result of parental upbringing, and any problem, from bed-wetting to schizophrenia, was laid at the feet of parents. If my brother had been born just 20 years ago, the approach to his disturbances would have been far different, looked at through the lens of neuro-scientific discoveries and advancements in research regarding child development and learning disabilities. The blame for his difficulties would not have been placed upon our parents so severely, and new and more effective ways of helping my brother learn to cope with life would have been available. As well, they would have had the benefit of excellent insights into the kind of discipline that yields results, so easily discussed now but considered private then.

But since these insights were not available, my parents did what they could with the knowledge they had. They could not separate my brother's actions from their shame at producing such a son, nor from their love for him. They had no one to talk to who understood the complexity of what was going on and could explain it to them. There was no one who could accurately diagnose his symptoms, no Internet they could search to discover treatments for my brother's torment, few support groups where they could identify with other parents who faced the same challenges.

In the 1950s, psychologist John Bowlby coined the term "attachment disorder" and wrote of his work with children who suffered from it, but he was not some famous man my mother might have read about in a women's magazine. Who in my parents' world could explain what was going on? Tried-and-true child-rearing methods and advice didn't work, and they must have been panicked by what this said of their parenting ability. My folks felt they should simply be able to handle the situation. This was a *child* they were dealing with! The prevailing wisdom was parents just needed to set a kid on the straight and narrow and stick to their guns.

Addressing this loss of confidence parents of troubled children often face, Jane Ryan wrote: "I have never met a guilt-ridden parent who was up to doing an adequate job of rearing their youngsters. When one feels bad about oneself as a parent or has a poor sense of self, then one's role as a parent becomes compromised. Without confidence in one's self or abilities, even the most minimal expectations in caretaking cannot be met."[4] Ryan knows what she is talking about. Her passion for the subject was born of necessity. One of her adopted children exhibited the most extreme symptoms of what is now called Reactive Attachment Disorder. After losing her marriage because of the disruptions her son created, losing two houses to the expense of therapies engaged to address his behaviors, nearly losing her sanity as her son set fires in the house, tortured family pets, ran away, threatened suicide—all of this before the age of 7—she finally had to place her 12-year-old son in a facility that could watch him around the clock. She then began a search for answers to her anguished questions. What made a child act in such a way? What experience could make a child so destructive, so inhuman? She was driven to find out what had gone wrong and it impelled her to study and research the conditions that formed her son. My parents didn't seem to *want* to know. To pursue causes or treatments was just . . . too hard. It took time and effort they could not muster. It was overwhelming.

I can't be sure my brother would have been diagnosed with Reactive Attachment Disorder, or something as severe. There are a number of ways to look at his behavior that just weren't as clear in childhood as they seemed when he became an adult. Perhaps clinicians would have assessed Danny as exhibiting the signs of Conduct Disorder. "Children and adolescents with this disorder have great difficulty following rules and behaving in a socially acceptable way," explains the website of the American Academy of Child & Adolescent Psychiatry.[5] Brain damage or genetic vulnerability can be contributing factors to this disorder, which simply underscores what I have already said—Danny's problems would be looked at in a different light today. In any event, whatever services might have been in existence to help him still required intention and effort. "Treatment," says the AACAP site, ". . . can be complex and challenging. . . . Parents often need expert assistance in devising and carrying out special management and educational programs in the home and at school."[6] The ruthless pursuit of answers, of programs that could have addressed the situation, was simply not part of my parents' makeup.

Were they "bad" parents? No. They were typical parents, like other men and women doing the very best they can out of sincere and gripping love for their children, but often drawing only upon the inadequate examples of how they themselves were raised. Parenting classes in the 1950s and 1960s were largely psychoanalytical lessons for the layperson with little practical application. The books, courses, social services, support groups, counselors, and organizations dedicated to assisting families that are available today just weren't around then.

There wasn't a lot of help available, but they wouldn't take advantage of even the little that existed. By the time my brother was a teenager, an Al-Anon group met weekly at a nearby church. The "Tough Love" program was just beginning around then, meeting in our neighborhood. I'd plead with them to attend an Al-Anon meeting with me or challenge them to check out the Tough Love instruction. They wouldn't. They preferred to close the doors and windows and insist they could take care of things. It was a lie they told themselves, and we all lived with the consequences of it.

In her book, Jane Ryan showcases the story of parents Troy and Leslie, she a licensed vocational nurse with a master's degree in social work and he a registered nurse with a Ph.D. in neuropsychology. This California couple adopted a child whose conduct rings with familiarity for me. Life with their son, reported Leslie, "was chaos and struggle from the moment he got up in the morning 'til he went to bed at night." He would threaten them: "When I get big, I'm going to come back and kill you." In interviews, Troy told Jane Ryan of the way their child could get what he wanted: "He can read your facial expressions, your gestures . . . like he has some kind of radar; he can size up your weaknesses, what bothers you, whatever. He can read people very quickly and if he chooses to can provoke them or manipulate them in some fashion."[7]

Here were two educated, knowledgeable parents who found life with their child overwhelming. They did everything they knew to do before acknowledging they could do no more, finally placing their boy in residential psychiatric care. "Many of their young son's behaviors did not make sense to the parents, both experts in the mental health field. It appeared to Troy and Leslie that their son moved from one mess to another, all of his own making."[8] These parents saw that conventional parenting methods would not work. They knew the problem was bigger than they were. They did what they could and when efforts were fruitless, sought help. If two highly trained professionals could not deal with such a child, is it any wonder my parents could not? Rather than admitting they were powerless to handle my brother and needed help, my folks took responsibility to an extreme and carried their burden alone.

After my father was diagnosed with Alzheimer's disease and came to live with my husband and me, he constantly brought up my brother as he slipped in and out of the past. "He was on self-destruct his whole life. I feel so sorry for him. My poor, poor son. I tried to help him in every way I could." He asked me at dinner one evening if I thought that being born premature might have damaged Danny's brain, that this might be why he never "made it in life." I told him yes, of course—Danny was developmentally disabled, to a degree. "But he wasn't mentally incompetent, Dad," I said. I kept silent, thinking of all of the ways my father had helped him remain on self-destruct. I finally said, "Danny was very smart in some ways," and he looked at me with surprise. "He figured out how to get exactly what he wanted," I told him, and with that my father returned to his plate, speechless.

Even now, I have to dodge the memories that clutch at my heart and cause me to cry out with grief. What kind of family would we have been without the scourge of drugs and alcohol? What if my brother had been born fully developed with all of his faculties intact? What would have happened if my parents had handled things differently? These are questions I cannot dwell on because they have no answers. I can't imagine anything different than what we lived through. I only know what did happen and what became of all of us, and how the grace of God both preceded us and followed us through our lives and managed to do its powerful work in spite of the challenges we threw at it.

I can now recognize the grace that worked in our lives, but for much of my life it was hard to see any evidence of the hand of the Lord. I felt trapped and afflicted by forces far outside my control while tragedy fermented in the house in which I lived. My heart still breaks over the memory of wasted opportunities, wasted time, wasted energies. I didn't have a healthy family. My parents weren't abusers, we didn't live in poverty, and I wasn't denied an education; my life was far better than many people I've met. Nevertheless we were sick—sick with pretense, with secrets everyone knew; sick with emotional and spiritual parasites that ate away at hope and joy and right relationships.

My story can remain one of tragedy and sadness, or it can be redeemed. I grew up in a sick family and yet have grown to be whole and healthy. This is the unfathomable grace of God! Oh, I could assert I am wiser, I am stronger, I am more grounded, but I have known many smart and well-equipped men and women who've lived their lives forever stalked by the shadows of their pasts. It takes the power of the Lord Jesus Christ to break free of the web created by my family life. It takes the eye of the Master to see the value of His creation and draw a person through the very experiences that, while having the potential to imprison them, can ultimately set them free.

CHAPTER THREE

Journey to a Distant Land

If we do not transcend nature, we remain bound to the people we cannot forgive, held in their vise grip. This principle applies even when one party is wholly innocent and the other wholly to blame, for the innocent party will bear the wound until he or she can find a way to release it—and forgiveness is the only way.

PHILIP YANCEY [1]

"You're adopted." My mother shrank back into the driver's seat and pressed herself hard against the door, as though willing herself to disappear. We were sitting in the car in the driveway after a shopping spree at J.C. Penney. My new baby-blue luggage was in the back of the station wagon, along with the clothes I was going to take with me to West Virginia where I would be spending the summer with relatives, my last significant contact before relationships were lost to years of separation. The trip was a gift for my 14th birthday, coming up in a few weeks.

We pulled up to the house and Mom turned off the ignition. As I reached to open the door, she told me to wait. "I have something to tell you," she said, her voice trembling. She took a couple of deep breaths and then blurted out the secret she feared would start some kind of emotional nuclear reaction. I took in her words for just a moment, staring first at the dashboard and then at her. Seeing the tears in her eyes, I realized I did not have the luxury of digesting this information until later. I had to act swiftly before she had a meltdown. I reached across the seat and grabbed her hand. "Mommy, that's wonderful!" Her eyes widened. "Just think," I continued, "you chose me! I think that's really neat! Really!"

She searched my face to see if I was being truthful and then nearly sobbed with relief. "You . . . you don't *hate* me?" She had prepared herself for the worst. I leaned across the seat and put my arms around her, mentally processing the information I'd just been given and promising myself I'd ponder it when I was alone. I assured her again I thought it was simply *fantastic!*

"Why didn't you tell me before?" I asked. She explained that doctors had warned them not to tell me I was adopted until my 21st birthday, but because someone in the family might accidentally remark upon the circumstances of my birth, she and Dad had decided to tell me before my trip. The subject did come up that summer, and I was glad my mother had told me so I could react as though it was no big deal. In fact, it really *wasn't* a big deal. I knew no other family. I looked like I belonged.

Childhood pictures of my brother and me show a resemblance, and I was often told I took after a blonde aunt. In later years, people would tell me how I favored my mother, how obvious it was that I was her daughter.

I took some time after the revelation to ponder the announcement, and now that the secret was out my mother answered every question, eager to tell me all she knew. Every so often I'd wonder what birth parent I truly resembled. My mother was pretty sure my birth father had died shortly after I was born, and she was sorry she had no pictures. She urged me to be forgiving toward my birth mother, and continued to do so throughout the years. "Life was hard for her. She just couldn't cope with a baby," she would say. "She did the very best thing she could for you by leaving you with a friend. Don't ever hold it against her."

I didn't. I was what the psychological literature calls a "nonsearcher." I never had the searcher's feelings of incompleteness or dissatisfaction, the belief that I would never be whole until I found my "real" mother. It never felt necessary to touch the foundations of my life, seeking an answer to the big questions of my existence. Whatever insecurities or depressions or fears I had to deal with, I never connected them to needing to know my birth family.

My visit back East was filled with more than one significant event, the most important of which was my decision to become a Christian. I'd been raised in the Methodist church but had lately wanted to become a Catholic because I loved the solemnity and ritual of the Mass. After reading *The Nun's Story*, I had asked my mother if I could find a convent school to attend, and I had it in my mind that I'd take vows and join an order someday. I wanted to be religious and holy; nuns were both, so that worked for me! That summer, I was introduced to the idea that being a good religious person and being a true follower of Jesus are two different things. This was new to me.

For a year after returning home, I trudged up to the church on the corner and tried to do whatever it was I thought Christians were supposed to do. No one had instructed me or given me anything but a Bible and good wishes after I went forward in a Baptist church in South Charleston in response to the call to those who desired to follow Jesus—to become a follower not just by mental assent, but by a commitment of the heart. When I had asked what came next, I was told to just read my Bible and go to church. Because I had no one to guide me, I started reading the Bible at Genesis and plowed through the Old Testament, sneaking peeks at the New because, avid reader that I was, I didn't want to jump too far ahead and spoil the story! As you can imagine, I was pretty much worn out around the time I hit some of the endless genealogies that roll for pages on end. I could stick with attending services, though, and I walked to the neighborhood Baptist church Sunday after Sunday, sitting by myself, trying to hear something that would feed that deep-seated desire to know the Jesus Who had drawn me. I'd go and sit in my favorite Catholic Church sanctuary by myself, listening and waiting. I didn't know at the time what I was looking for; I only knew that something had happened to me and I needed to be where it felt like He might be, where people were talking about Him, even though I couldn't understand what they were talking about. I waited in the church pew every week, listening as though to a foreign language, thinking perhaps one day I would start recognizing words and phrases and eventually learn the lingo.

One Sunday morning, the youth group shared their experiences with the congregation after returning from church camp. I hadn't been to any of their meetings in the year I'd been attending services, but now I could see they were absolutely lit up with passion for the Lord, relating how their lives had been changed, how enthusiastic they were about Jesus Christ. My thirst for His presence was almost painful after hearing people who had experienced Him in this way and were excited to tell everyone that *God is real!* This was Southern California in 1971, the beginning of what was later called "The Jesus Movement," and in retrospect it seems like something gripped young people everywhere to search for whatever would fill the "God-shaped hole inside." It was also a time of charismatic renewal, and folks all over were finding themselves desperate for the deeper things of God, a desire for a relationship, not with church and religious activities but with the reason for church—the risen King of kings. I can only say the Spirit of God was moving in a particular way during that time, and it had touched the high school kids of the First Baptist Church of Westchester that summer of 1971. I saw it and wanted it with everything in me.

That evening in the youth meeting, received with joy and a welcome I had not been able to feel until then, I listened as they prayed to a real person, obviously someone they knew and loved, and I fell in love with Him too. The light came on and the eyes of my heart saw Him! I had invited Him into my life the summer before, not grasping the profound importance of my prayer. It was a year before my mind and my heart absorbed what had happened.

I had a glorious moment of truth—one that changed me forever—but continuing in the walk of daily life was a constant challenge. Making an intentional decision to become a Christian did not change the atmosphere of my home. I still lashed out at my brother in hatred and we fought as we always had. My relationship with my parents was chronically strained. A week did not go by without some catastrophe occurring. My parents were continually worn out from dealing with Danny. My father retreated into a shell and my mother tried to pull him out of it by berating him, hoping to cause a reaction.

I spent much of the next year asking the members of the church to pray for my family. Every Sunday evening when the pastor asked for prayer requests, I implored everyone to pray for my mom and dad. I can't imagine what these people thought of me: I spent my first year sitting on the sidelines, quiet and withdrawn; the second year I spent weeping in nearly every service, overwhelmed by the goodness of God, and constantly asking for prayer for my family.

"Keep on asking," said Jesus, and a marvelous thing occurred: within a year or two my parents also made decisions to follow the Lord! My mother was first. Dad could see evidence of what had happened to me and then couldn't deny the change in my mother. During a difficult hour when he was experiencing an emotional crisis, he allowed my mother to lead him in prayer, asking Jesus to come into his life and change him. I was overjoyed!

But the fact that the three of us had experienced a tremendous internal revolution had no effect upon my brother's behavior. He went to the altar for prayer a few times when my parents managed to get him into church. Later in life, he'd go through rehab and come out determined to change, claiming he'd dedicated his life to the Lord. When it was necessary for him to appease my parents, he played upon this most vulnerable part of them: their desire to see him set free and serving God. And many, many times, when they were straining toward that hope, believing with all their hearts that this was it—this time he'd really turned his life over and things would change—he would cruelly dash their hopes by relapsing in the most destructive way and laughing at them, mocking their faith and cursing God.

Everything he touched, every friendship he made, every connection he had was as sordid as he was. His friends were kids on drugs, kids who sold drugs, kids who were already criminals and with whom he joined in criminal activity. He participated in and was the object of the kind of destructiveness that he dismissed by claiming it was all "just a joke." He would have a falling out with "friends" and they'd respond like assassins. One day, one of his partners in crime drove up next to his car on a busy street and jumped out with a crowbar in hand and prepared to smash the window next to Danny's head. He managed to drive away before being assaulted but came home hysterical, claiming to be unaware of why anyone would want to hurt him. Mom and Dad joined in the panic although I was sure they couldn't honestly think he was innocent. Who was he kidding? He acted like an attempt on his life just came out of the blue. He was involved with any number of rotten people, and he'd made a few of them angry.

There were so many awful episodes involving my brother. There were guns and drugs, threats of murder and suicide, stealing and jail time. They run together and are lost to my specific recollection, but a few stand out as potent examples of the lunacy going on at home. For example, I'll never forget my senior prom because of what I came home to the morning after. Friends and I had gone together as a group and later delighted in the fun of showing up at an all-night bowling alley near our high school in our formal clothes to form teams and play several games. I drove home around 6:00 a.m., and as I turned the corner onto our street I could see the cars in our driveway: every one of their windows had been smashed. Glass covered the ground. I parked my car on the street and investigated the destruction before I entered the house, knowing that Danny's "friends" had done this sometime in the night. I stopped by my parents' room to tell them about the cars and then I went to bed.

I couldn't feel upset about things like this—not after so many years of witnessing every kind of extreme spectacle—and I couldn't understand why such incidents still had the power to send my mother into hysterics. I realize now, of course, that I turned off my feelings when it came to dealing with my family and placed myself above it all, outside of the little kingdom of mother, father, and son. It was the only way to protect myself. I could not endure the wild emotions going on at home. I hated the chaos, the same old fights, the same old shouting matches, and the same old resolutions to change.

When I draw on the memories of my family, it's not so much actual events I think of. I feel the thumbprint of pervasive depression, the heaviness of a family struggling to breathe. There were good things, and I try to focus on them. But the whole mess of it dwells in my head as a big, dark cloud. I remember feeling trapped. "It will always be like this," I'd think with despair, and then I'd get angry and would make plans to get away.

My parents would become fed up once in a while and they'd tell Danny he was being grounded, was having his car taken away, was not to go out. But they enforced nothing and he did as he pleased. It never ceased to anger me. I don't know why I couldn't simply accept the truth about my family. I was just too young, I guess. I hadn't learned how hard it is for people to change, how painful it is to look at one's self and admit culpability. I couldn't know how my parents' emotions were twisted up with Danny, impossible to untangle. He wanted to hurt them. Something in him hated them while loving them, and he was perennially outraged at them for something even he could not explain. He loved them and needed them, but cursed them for being foolish enough to expect him to be anything but what he was. In his most desperate moments he cried out for them to rescue him and once they did, he spit in their faces, sometimes literally.

This is my personal example of the younger son of Jesus' parable. He demanded his inheritance of my parents in ways that are almost too painful for me to recount. He demanded their lives. He demanded they sacrifice all to him, and when they complied he hurt them as deeply as he knew how. My brother played upon their guilt, used it, manipulated them with great skill as addicts and alcoholics know intuitively how to do. All he had to do was shout at my dad, "You were never a father to me," and he would be given whatever he demanded. He could play my mother like she was his private puppet, telling her whatever she wanted to hear, knowing her great hope for his salvation. He would get the money he required or the silence he demanded and then he would go off, defying them to discipline him. Until he died at the age of 43, he threw tantrums, hurling insults and screaming obscenities, crying like a 2-year-old, fuming like a sullen teenager.

And I, the "older son" standing on the sidelines of our family, watched it all. I was the good child. I waited to be acknowledged.

I did well, hoping to make them proud, but they rarely had the time or energy to acknowledge me because their lives were consumed with him. Every time they gave my brother support they could not afford, I wondered anew just how much they had spent on him over the years and if I'd ever see its equal, and then I'd feel guilty for begrudging what they'd given him.

"Look!" said the older brother in Luke 15:29-30. "All these years I've been slaving for you and never disobeyed your orders. Yet you never gave me even a young goat so I could celebrate with my friends. But when this son of yours who has squandered your property with prostitutes comes home, you kill the fattened calf for him!" I understand that furious howl, because my parents gave the "fattened calf" to my brother over and over. I understand the resentment the older brother lived with. I know what creates it and how it is nurtured.

That does not excuse my inability to hope for my brother as my parents did, but my brother did not return in repentance either. He never said to my parents, "I have sinned against God and against you. I am no longer worthy to be called your son." After a certain point, I never held any hope or even any desire to see my brother change, and sometimes I conveniently forgot I had a brother. I just wanted him to go away. Every time he left home, there was a period of quiet respite, but within a week or two my mother was pacing the floor, praying, crying, wanting him home; my father was sleepless and depressed. Months would pass and my brother would return, usually in some terrible condition, and while I knew my parents were relieved he was alive, the cycle would start again. Someone said insanity is continuing to the do the same thing while expecting different results, and I watched as the things that had never worked were tried time and time again. I felt like I'd find more tranquility in a psychiatric unit. Every moment he was present was filled with the potential for turmoil and destruction. One time, during a period when he was sober and communicative, I took him out to lunch and begged him to go away and leave Mom and Dad in peace. In desperation,

I told him I'd send him whatever money I could if he would just stay away and let them have a quiet retirement, free of the worry his behavior brought. I wanted my parents to have a life. I wanted them to experience something they'd never had since his childhood—a time when there was no crisis, no phone call in the middle of the night, no destruction of property, no theft, no tantrums. But my brother could not do it, and it was not what my parents wanted anyway.

I, the prodigal brother, began the journey at an early age to a distant land inside the heart. My parents' actions plainly indicated they were grateful I was no trouble so they could expend themselves upon my brother. I felt immense rage at their foolishness every time they gave him money, knowing he would spend it immediately and before long be back for more. The sick helplessness I'd experience when my parents allowed my brother to bludgeon them with guilt, when they'd rush to his side and bail him out of jail, when they'd tell me that their responsibility as parents was to support him no matter what, would send me to some quiet place where I could sob out my agitation and pain at the awful drama being played out every day. I felt like an outsider in my own family. I left home immediately after high school and was usually reluctant to return, because within minutes of my arrival the discussion of my brother's most recent activities would begin. They wanted my advice. They couldn't know how it infuriated me that they would ask because I knew it would never be heeded.

Their lives were a paradox. They gave godly advice and counsel to many people. They could persuade the most down-and-out characters looking for a new beginning to think before acting on some decision and wait before proceeding down a particular path. In spite of all my frustration, I am deeply grateful for my parents. I can gladly talk for hours about their wonderful attributes. My mother was a tremendous soul-winner who truly loved people. A marvelous storyteller, she was fascinated by the family histories and life stories of those she befriended. My father adored children and animals. He would do anything to avoid hurting people's feelings, no matter what his opinion of their appearance or actions. Both of them were always generous. Deeply compassionate people, their hearts were sweet wells and they seemed to attract the weak, helping them on their journeys. Many are the times they paid someone's electric bill, or bought groceries for a single mother facing a rough patch, or helped finance a car for a struggling young believer. They taught me lasting values. They gave me a good work ethic, taught me to pay my bills on time, and helped me be true to my word.

But my dad could not take advice from others, no matter how reputable the source, and he made countless unwise, impulsive decisions. He saw himself as the "poor relation" in his family and was insecure around them, and this insecurity fed a pride that led him to consistently reject solid counsel. My mother often arrived at conclusions after following the most illogical path and then wondered why she wasn't taken seriously. She could react to stressful events with emotional extremes, falling easily into the role of the persecuted martyr. With the many good things they had and the friends they shared at a more happy time in their lives, they moved along heedlessly until late in life they ended up living in a mobile home in a hopeless little town, barely getting by on Social Security checks, raising my nephew because my brother was incapable of being a father.

How I wish things could have been different! How I wish there could have been a moment of truth when my precious parents, so whipped and worn by the circumstances of life, could have seen a light and changed their direction. How I wish I could have rid myself of my awful judgment and looked upon the whole, pathetic mess with some tenderness, with a sympathy that would have washed over my sorrow and healed the hole in my heart. "Out of the depths I cry to you, O LORD; O Lord, hear my voice. Let your ears be attentive to my cry for mercy" (Psalm 130:1-2). I didn't have much mercy on them. May God have mercy on me.

"Can the elder son in me come home?" asked Henri Nouwen in his priceless book *The Return of the Prodigal Son*. "How can I return when I am lost in resentment, when I am caught in jealously, when I am imprisoned in obedience and duty lived out as slavery?"[2] I want to present myself as the highly compassionate, understanding child who gave of herself without reservation to a family that seemed to implode at regular intervals—but I wasn't. I was angry about it, and remained angry and carried my anger with me into adulthood. How many times I've tried to look back at my history with eyes of holy insight, bearing all things, believing all things, hoping all things. How many times I have been pierced with disappointment in myself when I become aware of how deeply the roots of my judgment have burrowed. Nouwen continues: "I cannot be reborn from below; that is, with my own strength, with my own mind, with my own psychological insights. There is no doubt in my mind about this because I have tried so hard in the past to heal myself from my complaints and failed . . . and failed . . . and failed, until I came to the edge of complete emotional collapse and even physical exhaustion."[3]

Only Jesus can bring us to the place of ridding ourselves of this internal poison that threatens to choke all God is working in us. Only Jesus can help us take His hand so He can walk us to the house where the party is going on. It's that hand extended we must respond to. There is a way to get to forgiveness. There is a journey to making peace with all that's happened. Does it feel impossible? Sometimes our burden is so great it seems we need the Father, who has run to meet us, to pick us up and carry us through the door, and if that would accomplish something I'm sure He would do it. We must walk through that door, but the Father has hold of our hands, drawing us like a parent helping a child with its first steps, urging us to leave the land of our anger and cross the threshold to forgiveness and freedom.

— CHAPTER FOUR —

I Used to Be a Pharisee

Now the tax collectors and "sinners" were all gathering around to hear him. But the Pharisees and the teachers of the law muttered, "This man welcomes sinners and eats with them."

—LUKE 15:1-2

I was a contemptuous, condescending adolescent who had barely a shred of respect for my parents. I thought I knew so much. I thought I had the answers to my parents' lack of parenting ability, and the truth is all I had was an intense desire for my brother to disappear. I hated the regular eruptions of turmoil in our home. I hated that the neighbors could hear the screaming and the fighting and the cussing. I hated when my brother made a scene in the driveway or the police drove up to the house. I hated there was never any true *peace*. The peace that would settle over our home was a tense, miserable, what-else-is-there-to-say quiet with an episode of "Bonanza" playing on the television in the den, where a stressed-out mother and father sat in worried silence. I retreated to my room—to my telephone, my TV, my books, my journals, and my music. I cut myself off from them emotionally, taking every opportunity to remind the three of them that *I was different!*

I was lonely. I felt set apart in my own family. I imagine this is how the older son of Jesus' story felt as he surveyed the events that carried on with abandon in front of him. Who invited him in? Who noticed he was missing? As the father embraced his weary, travel-scarred child, did he turn and say to a servant, "Quick! Find my older son so I can share this news with him and we can rejoice together!"? It was as though the older brother did not exist except as an afterthought. All of life was about the younger son.

The footnote in my *NIV Study Bible* says this of the parable: "The forgiving love of the father symbolizes the divine mercy of God, and the older brother's resentment is like the attitude of the Pharisees and teachers of the law who opposed Jesus."[1] At face value, this is certainly one of the things Jesus was saying to a listening group of tax collectors, sinners, and teachers of the law. In his book, *What's So Amazing About Grace?*, Philip Yancey explains that as the Pharisees watched Jesus' behavior and the people with whom he associated—tax collectors, prostitutes, no-accounts—they "had trouble swallowing the notion that these are the people God loves. At the very moment Jesus was captivating the crowd with his parables of grace, Pharisees stood at the edges of the crowd muttering and grinding their teeth. In the story of the Prodigal Son, provocatively, Jesus brought in the older brother to voice proper outrage at his father for rewarding irresponsible behavior."[2] The older son was the voice of the hardcore Pharisee.

I have a personal image of a Pharisee that speaks to me, one from my favorite Christmas movie. In the 1947 film "The Bishop's Wife," Cary Grant plays Dudley, an angel sent to assist Bishop Henry Brougham, played by David Niven. Henry is the pastor to the wealthy and fashionably religious people of his community, and he expects the answer to his prayer for help will be a heavenly messenger who can bring him the funds he needs to build the cathedral he has designed—for God's glory, he insists. But it is soon clear that Henry isn't honest with himself, because it's not lost on anyone he believes erecting the church will establish his reputation and bring him respect.

The desire for recognition has turned Henry into a morose, angry man who neglects his wife and child to tend to the affluent society matrons who can provide the money for his dream if he will only grovel enough. Loretta Young plays his wife, Julia, who tries to pull him back to the time when he was real, a time when they were poorer in material things but rich in friends and the treasures of life, when building a relationship was more important than building a sanctuary.

In comes Dudley, who transforms everything simply by entering a room. He brings a touch of frivolity to his interactions with people. Everyone wants to be around Dudley! The prim secretary wears a flower in her hair, knowing that Dudley will notice and compliment her. The housekeeper offers him a scarf to wear in the cold of a winter day, one she had given to the bishop, who never used it; Dudley displays it with style. The cab driver comes looking for him because being with Dudley is when he feels most alive. Children connect with him because he seems to see the world from their point of view. Even Professor Wutheridge, an old intellectual who has let his dreams slip through his fingers, senses there is something different about Dudley. Henry, though, is supremely annoyed with every facet of Dudley's personality and prays fervently for him to leave!

But the heavenly administrators apparently want Dudley to stay put for a little while. My favorite scene is one in which he visits an arrogant old battleaxe of wealth and power, Mrs. Agnes Hamilton. She is Henry's moneybags, the one who can single-handedly fund his temple of admiration—if only he will leave God's name out of it and dedicate it to the memory of her dead husband, George. Henry has finally succumbed, desiring his cathedral at any cost. He and Julia are on their way to meet with her when Dudley shows up unexpectedly at Mrs. Hamilton's home, asking for an audience.

He waits for her in her drawing room, searching with his spiritual senses for the one bit of important information he knows will hold the key to everything she's become. He finds it, locked up and preserved: a piece of music written for the harp, inscribed to her with love, not by her late husband, George, but by a man named Allen. Dudley positions himself at the harp and begins to play the composition.

Mrs. Hamilton hears it from the top of the stairs and is almost overcome with emotion as the music her true love wrote for her fills the house. She makes her way to the room and stands, watching him play, transfixed. When the music is over, Dudley smiles and takes her hand, alludes simply to the truth she has hidden away, leads her to the couch, and compels her to share with him the deepest secrets of her heart. "Tell me," he says gently, brimming with empathy and kindness, as though he has always known her and was expecting this very opportunity to hear her reveal her soul.

Agnes can't tell her story fast enough. She had known passion—"the only man I ever loved"—for a musician who was poor, but was unable to bring herself to marry him because poverty frightened her. She fled into marriage with her husband, a staggeringly wealthy man who was crazy for her, and then simmered in guilt over her cowardice and dishonesty, her heart slowly hardening. She became cold, demanding, joyless, working hard to maintain the illusion she loved the man she married. "I've spent a fortune building monuments to his memory," she tells Dudley, and breaks down in his arms.

Shortly thereafter, Henry and Julia arrive and are ushered into a room to wait for her. A tense silence has settled between them; Julia has sadly resigned herself to the price Henry has paid for his desire. But when Mrs. Hamilton enters the room, they are astonished to find her a changed woman! They don't know quite how to respond to this new creature, this gracious person who has been drained of her dark and haughty superiority. She had been able to unburden herself to Dudley. He didn't even need to tell her she had been walking the wrong way through the traffic of life; *she* told *him*. His warmth and genuine interest in Agnes gave her permission to admit her own sins. She's free! An unexpected smile makes her look younger. She tells Julia, "Meeting Dudley has been the greatest spiritual experience of my life!" She tops it off with the stunning announcement that she no longer wants to give any of her vast fortune to the building of the cathedral. She now desires to distribute it to the poor and needy and wants Henry to see it is done properly.

Throughout the movie, Mrs. Hamilton exudes the character of a Pharisee, a designation that has taken on a life of its own over the centuries. Just as the name of Ebenezer Scrooge of Charles Dickens' *A Christmas Carol* is a synonym for a cheap and money-obsessed person, "Pharisee" has become a synonym for a self-righteous, pompous man or woman who presumes to speak for God or the establishment, who sees himself or herself as better than others, annoyed with those who aren't as enlightened or as holy, irritated with anyone who seeks to change the status quo.

The Pharisees aren't the stuff of fiction, though, as were Scrooge and Agnes Hamilton. They were real people, men committed to the Word of God, pledging to be examples of devotion to the

Law of Moses and the memory of their patriarchs. In a time long before Jesus of Nazareth when the Jewish people had assimilated into Greek culture without a backward glance, the Pharisees rose up as beacons for the ways of their forefathers who had spoken of a time when the Lord would once again gather His people to Himself and make them great, setting over them the Holy One of Israel, the Messiah.

I particularly love "The Bishop's Wife" because Dudley matches my conception of what Jesus must have been like: someone who saw deep into the heart, past the defenses and the masks, and wasn't shocked. A man who made people feel special just by the way He looked at them, as though they shared some delightful secret. A person with whom folks felt compelled to share their most intimate fears and private longings, who received from Him an infusion of confidence and a hope for the future. This is the man who can lead a Pharisee from the work of monument-making to the couch of tender memories to have her rise up changed, freed, with a new vision of purpose and filled with His abundant life.

The thing is, I've always found myself attracted to the zeal of the Pharisees. They had such a glowing purpose, a rock-solid philosophy. They did not take the words of God lightly. I love that! They believed with forceful assurance that sin was not to be tolerated. They knew the very least sin could prevent blessings from the hand of God. They knew the words of the prophets who had proclaimed the Lord was merciful, compassionate, slow to anger, quick to forgive, but also unrelentingly holy. They knew the historical accounts that demonstrated how even seemingly minor sins meant nothing less than pure rebellion and brought ultimate disaster. The truth of sin, the Pharisees understood, was not that it was some excusable mishap God looked upon with indulgence and dismissive pardon, but was an indication of rebellion toward God. In his book with the pithy title, *The Pharisees' Guide to Total Holiness*, William Coleman wrote that "it would be unfair to try to reduce the Pharisees to a simple definition. To blithely declare that they were 'hypocrites' or 'unloving' or 'fanatics' fails to see their complexity and depth. . . . They considered their priorities close to the heart of God. The Pharisees had no greater task than to protect and propagate the laws of God."[3] We think of them as critical, inflexible judges of other people's behavior, but they didn't start out that way. These were men who felt it was necessary to take a stand for what was good and right and precious about God's laws. Coleman likens them to the Marines, looking for "a few good men" who could be shining lights among the people. What does it mean to "love the Lord with all your heart and with all your soul and with all your strength"? The Pharisees took the command seriously and wanted to live it every day.

By the time of Jesus, their name, meaning "separated ones," had become a title they wore with excessive pride, but it wasn't the kind of pride that signified respect and love for their heritage. It had become most evidently pride in their specialness, carrying the hubris of those who sincerely believed their affiliation made them better than others. They didn't want anything to thwart their standing and influence. They relished their symbols of identity—prayer shawls and tassels, loud prayers in conspicuous places, comments that broadcast their displeasure with what they saw around them. What they did and how it was perceived was of utmost importance. So in His stories and illustrations, Jesus rarely passes up a chance to expose the hypocrisy and misguided attitude of the Pharisees. He tells them directly they have neglected the intent of the Law. He excoriates the convoluted nature of their rules and how they have done nothing but create an empire of "sons of Abraham" that has virtually no connection to the Father. Jesus tells the story of two men who went to the temple to pray, one of them a Pharisee who proclaimed to God his worth, the other an outcast who begged the Lord for mercy. He informs the crowd that God accepted the second man and the Pharisee was rejected. How the blood pressure of nearby Pharisees must have risen when they heard such denunciations! How could it be possible that the Almighty would reject the man who fasted frequently and prayed openly? How impertinent to suggest that God would accept a man who repented with mere words!

Reading the Gospels, it is impossible to miss the arrogance of these men, their desire for public acknowledgment and respect, their complete lack of self-examining response to the charges Jesus made against them. We can almost feel them seething with anger after every exchange with Him. Believing they were doing everything required for the Lord's approval, the Pharisees considered it an act of fidelity to purposefully distinguish themselves from the "sinners" who did not adhere to the teachings they followed.

Over time, institutionalization beset the group. Following rules became more important than founding ideals and goals. Traditions took on greater significance than the reasons for those traditions. Outward behavior held greater value than inner commitment. For the Pharisees, the preservation and visibility of the group was a greater mandate than recognizing the One spoken of in their beloved Scriptures. Over the years, the goal shifted subtly from being seen by God as worthy to being seen by people as special, and this is where I can most identify with them.

After all, it is far easier to have specific rules by which to live than it is to have a simple, true relationship with the Lord and act as His Spirit leads us. We can read what He said in His Word, and we either believe it or we don't. We either know Him or we don't. Christians are to be about the business of knowing Him better, increasing our capacity to believe, seeking to understand more clearly as we seek first His kingdom and His righteousness—not checking to see if we (or others) are keeping up appearances. Jesus said we would be known by our fruit, by the behaviors and character produced by our relationship with Him, not by dedication to laws, codes, or commandments. As we grow, we are sure to behave in ways that other Christians find objectionable— Christians who have forgotten that they, too, didn't know "the rules" when they first met Jesus and came into the church, that they didn't see all things clearly right away, that God spoke to their hearts and minds and patiently showed them over time what was unproductive and how to discard it.

I think the Pharisees, as a membership organization, were attractive to personalities who needed to follow the letter of the law and make sure someone saw them and appreciated them for it. This is something I understand very well. When I made a decision to believe that Jesus is who He said He was and I committed myself to following Him and to seeking the truth He revealed, I was completely consumed with love for what I'd found. It was so real to me—*He* was so real to me—I wanted to do whatever it took to please Him, to delight Him with my conduct and my attitude. I, too, wanted to love the Lord with all my heart and soul and strength, whatever I thought that might entail. The problem was that I had a natural inclination to work in order to be seen and appreciated, and I translated pleasing the Lord into working to be perfect. As I took in the good things of the gospel, I began to make little monuments to my own goodness, my own ability to grasp what I forgot could not be grasped without His grace and mercy. My unclean motives twisted His intentions. Monument-building became a full-time job. I became a snob. I looked down with disgust upon those who couldn't see the truth like I did.

I thought I was helping God out by being loud and obvious about my faith, providing His light for others to see by. I didn't know how to be compassionate without a concern that I might condone something that offended God. I didn't know God did not need my protection! I thought I would be proving myself weak if I did not make sure others clearly understood what they were doing wrong, what they needed to do to get it *right*. Ensuring that others got things right meant something to me, but it sure didn't win me any friends. It's interesting, isn't it, that Jesus did not alienate sinners? They loved Him and wanted to be around Him. Other than the woman who had been caught in the act of adultery, to whom He said simply, "Go, and sin no more," we don't find Him chiding sinners for their behavior. It was the Pharisees He offended, and intentionally.

Maybe Jesus *did* talk to sinners about the changes they needed to make, but He could do it in a way that was truthful without being high-handed. Oswald Chambers said, "Jesus Christ never trusted human nature, yet He was never cynical, never suspicious, because He trusted absolutely in what He could do for human nature."[4] We've all known folks who have the gift of being able to say hard things to others without drawing blood. Not being cynical or suspicious or angry with others for not seeing the "right" way allows listeners to receive rebuke without being hit by hard criticisms of their actions. There is a distinct difference in a comment spoken by a man who offers it with tenderness while accepting us as we are, and one delivered by a man who spits it out harshly while holding us at arm's length.

Not understanding this, though, I became a performer, needing to show the Lord how truly I believed by trying to be perfect. I found myself falling down over and over, getting up each time more determined to get it right, thinking somehow the horrible stain of my inadequacies would be hidden by the color of my perfect conduct. I may have been saved by grace, by the undeserved favor of God; but by golly, grace was going to have nothing to do with my daily walk! I was going to prove I was spiritual by keeping every last law on the books. I look back now and realize that I saw God as a stern and rigid parent, as one busy with other, more important people than I. I worked to get His attention, to get answers to my prayers, to receive something from Him. I tended to look upon others with an air of disapproval, shaking my head at their senselessness, having no room for mistakes and failures. I might allow a few excuses for myself, because I knew I was taking all of the proper steps required for approval, but I allowed no one else any understanding and tenderness.

Jesus knows this heart attitude of the Pharisee today, just as He knew it then. He has a keen sense of our contaminated inner worlds; we cannot escape, just as the Pharisees of old could not stand to hear Him expose their motives so clearly. Some of them hated His sight—how accurately He saw into them—so much they couldn't bear for Him to live. They hated His eyes, His holy acumen that could see the inadequacy of their characters and the infection of sin in their souls. They had to find a way to snuff Him out. Phariseeism always looks to murder the offender, the one who exposes its motives and inadequacy.

"He upset their world," write John and Paula Sandford. "They had carefully built that system of proper behaviors to insure righteousness for themselves, and to ace out all the siblings who failed to perform as well as they. (The same is often true in the church today.) Along came Jesus and by His love and merciful flaunting of their Sabbath laws, told them that all their work-righteousness was to no avail. In no way could they feel His love—apart from rites and rituals. The alternative seemed emptiness. He was a menace. He undid them. Therefore they hated Him—and they still do today, even though they are born anew and naming His name in worship every Sunday in His Church!"

Jesus has to come and upset our worlds, the little universes we create to obtain the recognition we want so desperately. We may understand we don't merit His sacrifice, but we turn right around and try to prove our spirituality by keeping rules and regulations. We have such a hard time understanding it's free on both sides of the equation. We aren't saved by works we do and we aren't made spiritual by them, either. The Bible tells us we're to be heart-followers, loving from the depths of our souls, desiring to be completely identified with the righteousness of Christ. It requires an internal shattering of all we have built, and friends, this is not a painless process for those of us inclined to prove we've got what it takes. We don't have a thing worth trying to prove, and it can take one's entire life to stop trying and just enter into rest.

In the story of the prodigal son, the Pharisees were personified in the older brother, who was indignant with a father who would accept a sibling who had showed utter disrespect for law and tradition. Jesus skillfully exposed the arrogance of the Pharisees by revealing the disgust they held not just for a prodigal son, but also for a compassionate father! Until Jesus came to the end of the story, they were probably quite pleased with the highhanded response of the older son when he spat out, "This son of yours who has squandered your property with prostitutes," anticipating they would hear the contrite response of a father who had been brought to his knees by his wiser, morally superior son.

But Jesus ended the parable on a note they had not expected, and it must have confused many of them who heard. The point of most of the stories Jesus told was often lost on men who were raised in a culture that rewarded appearances over honesty and forgiveness. They couldn't be truthful about their own motives and they certainly didn't forgive others for their infractions. Interestingly, my *NIV Study Bible* subtitles this passage, "The Parable of the Lost Son." Which lost son is the focus of the story? Looked at directly, it's the story of the prodigal son, the one who threw it all away and came back to the father with nothing. Looked at from a different angle, it's the story of the prodigal brother, the one who held on tightly—and also came to the father with nothing. As an "older brother," I must admit I have struggled with the notion that the older brother did what was right and the younger brother did what was wrong, and that's the moral of the story! It's hard sometimes, when you have shined up your "rightness," to read the words of Jesus in Matthew 23:26: "First clean the inside of the cup and dish, and then the outside will also be clean." What? If the outside looks clean, who cares what's on the inside? We Pharisees are all about the element of outward appearance, while God is all about the heart's role in the making of a holy exterior.

I think I can understand why the Pharisees couldn't hear what Jesus was saying. They had done all of the right things and they believed that should mean something. Like anyone, after following the rules they wanted a reward. The problem was that God wasn't looking for the hard, shiny outside—the rule-follower. He wanted the pliable, vulnerable inside, the heart-follower, no matter how unkempt or unclean. When the inside is changed by the presence of the Holy Spirit, the outside starts to shine on its own. This is very hard to grasp when one has worked so hard, performed so well, and received only a perfunctory pat on the head. We want big hugs, stares of awe at our exceptional abilities, hands clutched to the heart with exclamations of approval and praise. We want a party thrown in our honor!

In the end, that compassionate father, the kind of father Jesus was trying to show His listeners, saw the heart of both of his children. He not only celebrated the return of the one for whom he stood watching—the one who expected to be sent to work as a servant, who saw himself as utterly cut off from all to which he had once belonged—he also tried to win the other son's heart with compassion. He did not leave the older son outside, saying, "Well, forget him! If he can't be happy for his brother and for me, he can just spend the night outside." No, he went out and appealed to his son's sense of fairness, of reason, of truth, of what was right. "See it with my eyes," the father urged his son.

Jesus tells us the father said, "But we had to celebrate and be glad, because this brother of yours was dead and is alive again; he was lost and is found." I feel those words in my heart, which, like the older son's, was hot with bitterness and pain. I am a lost son, too. Over the years, the Father has patiently and tenderly urged me to see my judgments and give them up so that I can rejoice with the rest of the house. Standing outside may have its value in letting others know how offended I am. Maybe I'm punishing them a little bit, too, placing a wedge between us, seeking to spoil their good time. They have to look out that window occasionally and see me, pacing, shivering, refusing to satisfy my hunger on principle, while I hope they recognize just how wrong they are. But what does it win me? The victory of causing others to feel guilty? The satisfaction of having no table at which to sit, no wine and cheese and bread eaten in fellowship with joyful family and friends? What stupidity! All of the energy I put into remaining offended could be so much better expended dancing by the fire. To tell you the truth—it's cold out here.

— Chapter Five —

Dancing As Fast As I Can

Our development, and its emotional refueling, depends on a reconciling interchange of give and take, in which our offers to be of use are recognized and accepted. To detach ourselves from all that we desired from our parents cannot help but cripple our unfolding.

—PETER SHABAD[1]

I remember the title of a book that signifies how I often felt growing up: *I'm Dancing As Fast As I Can*. That phrase appeals to me as a description for what motivated me as a child. I danced and danced and danced for attention and affection. "Performance orientation does not mean one who works hard, but one who works hard for the wrong reasons," explain John and Paula Sandford in *The Transformation of the Inner Man*. "A free person may work harder, in the same works—impelled only by love. Performance-oriented people require constant affirmation (unconsciously demanding it, sometimes verbally)."[2] That was me. I was oriented to perform, working for the wrong reasons.

If no one was watching as we grew up, we need to be sure someone is watching now. In order to get through to adulthood, we put on our worker's hat and stomped around doing all the right things hoping someone would see, and we created a script that we can't stop rehearsing even today because, as the Sandfords write, "we fear dying to that world of control we have falsely come to believe guarantees us belonging and love." The key word here is "falsely," because the control we exert doesn't truly make us belong or feel loved. It's simply better than feeling out of control. It's notable the older brother of the story was out working in the field when the younger child returned home. We Pharisees don't mind hard work as long as we know it might garner an award for "Best Performance in a Leading Role." In work, we have some sort of control.

There's nothing wrong with seeking attention and affection. In and of itself, the desire for attention is not right or wrong. But it can become a hindrance if we do not get the appreciation we crave—the attention of the people we love the most. Too often, parents see this natural tendency in their children and try to squelch what they fear is a penchant for being a "show-off," the forerunner of conceit and unflattering pride. If parents don't recognize the temperamental, internally hardwired needs of their children, they can step on precious components of individual personality.

Kids who are dutiful and industrious need to be appreciated. Children who are compliant and easygoing need to have their wishes and desires respected. Little ones who are serious and thoughtful require sensitivity. And the boy or girl who is a natural ham needs applause and accolades. Let them be drama kings and queens! Life will temper their proclivities. Tell them all how fabulous they are *just* as they are and try to prevent yourself from showing them how exasperated you are they're so . . . *themselves.* They sense your disapproval and it can set into motion that desire to find a way to please you even if it means forcing themselves into unnatural poses and responses. This unfortunate condition continues when they establish a relationship with God and they scramble to find a way to please Him. There can be no rest when we are not assured we are accepted as we are.

I performed, emotionally speaking, first because it came naturally to me, then because I thought it could obtain for me what I craved—attention—and finally because it was all I had to offer. But no matter how fast I danced, what I had to give wasn't what my parents noticed. By the time I entered adulthood, performing was an ingrained behavior, woven tightly into my approach to life. I am the older brother who believed doing things right would get me somewhere, and the extreme attention my not-right brother received twisted me into knots as I attempted to understand the kind of world in which egregious behavior was rewarded over and over with time, money, and energy. This is not fair, I thought. *If I act right, do right, I will be rewarded. I will be seen. Isn't that the way it works?* Before too long, I saw the whole universe full of foolish people who did not understand the way things were *supposed* to be. When one performed well, one was supposed to be recognized, respected, acknowledged, and . . . loved.

In the book of Acts, we are told there were "believers who belonged to the party of the Pharisees" (15:5). These men were demanding that Gentile believers follow the Law in order to be counted as brothers and sisters. How telling was Peter's response to them: "Now then, why do you try to test God by putting on the necks of the disciples a yoke that neither we nor our fathers have been able to bear?" (Acts 15:10). It may take the unbearable burden of striving for what Paul in Philippians referred to as "legalistic righteousness" before we finally understand there is no bigger and better reward waiting up ahead for working to prove our worthiness. If we don't grasp the powerful truth that righteousness was given to us without our having to perform for it, that we maintain that righteousness by staying focused on who Jesus is and what He did for us, we will fall into the awful trap of dancing to a row of empty chairs.

The Apostle Paul's detractors were angered by his continual rejections of rule-following. They were so incensed with what they perceived as disrespect for his heritage they poured their energies into having him arrested. He asked his Jewish brothers in the faith why they directed their zeal to the old practices instead of the new life: "Since you died with Christ to the basic principles of this world, why, as though you still belonged to it, do you submit to its rules: 'Do not handle! Do not taste! Do not touch!'? These are all destined to perish with use, because they are based on human commands and teachings. Such regulations indeed have an appearance of wisdom, with their self-imposed worship, their false humility and their harsh treatment of the body, but they lack any value in restraining sensual indulgence" (Colossians 2:20-23). We don't want just the *appearance* of wisdom; we want real, honest-before-God wisdom! Rules have no power to free us, no energy to impel change. Paul walked boldly into a world of paganism and idolatry when he began his ministry to the Gentiles, and you don't read of him laying into them with rules and regulations and demands for compliance. Instead, we see his desire to persuade men and women that Jesus could set them free from all of the human desires and destructions that bound them.

When dying people walk into our churches, shall we hand them The Book of Rules or The Word of Life? We were once perishing—did The Book of Rules unlock our prison of decay? How will anyone know what a true Christian looks like if we clothe ourselves in the same garb dead people are wearing—demands for achievement, the craving of titles and position, the expectation of reward for performing in the burdensome play of "Look at me, I'm doing it right!"? If Jesus came to give us rest from anything, it is this treadmill of requirements.

We might proclaim to others—and to ourselves—that we are simply submitting humbly to God by following the proper protocol when what we are truly looking for is to be considered righteous for what we have done. The Father loved us when we had done nothing to deserve His attention, and we head in the wrong direction when we start performing to get it. Paul said such thinking was "false humility." It might look something like humility, but it's really a play for respect. Humility is recognizing there's not a thing I can do to deserve God's favor, so I might as well submit to the fact that He loves me! False humility looks for recognition. It has no power to truly conquer sensual desires, impure thoughts and actions, and wrong motives. It simply dresses up performance in a cloak of godliness.

Step by step, as one walks with the Holy Spirit, eyes will be opened to the futility of various behaviors and thoughts, and those impurities will be set aside because they are no longer appealing instead of being stifled and hidden because they are unacceptable to the eyes of the group. As Christians we are to model the behaviors and the thinking of a free and redeemed people who look to the Bible as our operating manual. The truth of the gospel is not contained in what Paul referred to as "disputable matters," but in those that are without dispute: exhibiting the fruit of the Spirit. Living according to the law of the Spirit of life. Rejecting the expression of our sinful nature. Once sanctification is a reality within us, our hearts desire more and more truth. We can't force others to want truth or to desire life. We're responsible for our own desires for these things.

Paul could write with knowledge and conviction about the life-giving properties of God's kingdom because he had been raised in the monument-building kingdom of the Pharisees. They simply couldn't understand this kind of freedom. Perhaps they started out with it. Maybe at the beginning, when men were dismayed with the corruption and assimilation they saw all around them. Maybe at the beginning, when they longed for the strength of purpose and commitment to the God of their fathers of which they read in the Scriptures.

"There were many great and noble Pharisees, as a careful reading of the New Testament will verify," writes William Coleman. "In fact, after studying them, it is easy to see why many practicing Jews still treat the title with respect and honor. Christians need to hear more of the excellent contributions made by an organization that at times excelled in courage and character."3 While not all the Pharisees were the horrible creatures we've made them out to be, they did become the carriers of the jailer's keys. Satan is not satisfied only with capturing and imprisoning people who don't know the Lord's gift of life. "The one purpose of his heart," say Brent Curtis and John Eldredge in *The Sacred Romance*, "is the destruction of all that God loves, particularly his beloved."4 He is the Devourer, the Accuser, and he must destroy even the newest of believers if at all possible by convincing them that what Jesus did is not enough: they must do more, be more, work more, prove more emphatically that they are free—and their freedom goes up in smoke. When we burden the children of God with legalistic rules instead of principles for living, we are Pharisees.

As a group, the Pharisees danced for God, looking for that giant nod of approval and attention they thought they couldn't get any other way. But attention and approval is not what our souls ultimately need. What we need is to be set free, to be given a new heart, to become a new creature altogether! Philip Yancey says, "The gospel is not at all what we would come up with on our own."5 We want the Good News to be about us, about how well we perform, about how much we deserve what the Lord is offering. It's not. It's about God and His compassion for a creation that has rarely been able to fully capture what He's been after. In the parable of the lost son, Jesus let His listeners know, loud and clear, what God was after.

The older son would have gotten twice the inheritance of the younger son because in the Jewish culture, as well as other cultures of that part of the world, it was the right of the firstborn to receive a double portion of the inheritance (Deuteronomy 21:17). We know the older son received his inheritance at the same time because Jesus said when the younger son requested his, the father "divided his property between them." It was common for a father to do this, even years before he died, but that the younger son demanded it departed from custom. The older son had gotten twice what the younger brother had received, so what was he so angry about? Why play sour grapes? Why not join in the party when his brother returned and say, "Welcome home"?

He might have remained in his father's house, the house in which he grew up, out of duty. We tend to regularly read the meaning of "duty" as some obligation we must fulfill even though we don't want to. The common use of the word has changed significantly in the last hundred years. Duty used to have a positive connotation. It meant moral obligation, something one does simply because it is right. Morality has become relative to the person interpreting it and the idea of obligation has been worked on until it is frequently regarded as a commitment to oneself. But to the Jews, "duty" was not a word to be sneezed at. Duty was a visible expression of respect and, yes, love. One loved the Lord and thus followed the Law. One believed and respected the precepts and principles and showed it by dutiful commitment. Consider the history of the United States: the word "duty" means something different today than what it meant during the time of our Civil War. Reading the letters and diaries and comments of men and women from both North and South, I've noted how frequently the word "duty" is used to explain a passion to defend and protect what is precious. Today, we often discharge the word as though it signifies something we must do as the result of having our arms twisted.

It's true the older brother could have remained with his father out of an empty adherence to a law that had no meaning for him, or out of a desire for gain that fueled his false appearance of dedication. Or consider this: he could have loved his father. He could have seen the love his father had for his brother and wondered, as a diligent student of his people's history, "Why was the coat of many colors given to Joseph?" Why was Joseph's father so bonded to him when there were 11 others? Can any parent who knows the feeling truly explain why they have a more powerful or intense love for one child over another?

This is nothing new and unusual. As far back as the book of Genesis, we are told that "Isaac . . . loved Esau, but Rebekah loved Jacob" (Genesis 25:28). Parents want to treat siblings impartially, but our admirations are sometimes inexplicable. We may not be able to change our feelings, but we have moral obligations that speak louder than mere feelings. The father of the prodigal son may have been able to show his love for that son more readily, more openly, than he could for his older son. Maybe the father saw himself in the prodigal son. The older son may have felt that and longed for that special bond. We've all read stories (or have been a participant in one) in which a child cries out to mother or father, "I'm not just like you, but can't you love me anyway?" How difficult it can be to keep reaching out, seeking the evidence of a parent's love that is unable to connect with us. We shut down and move inside to stroke our wounds. Inside is where wonder gives way to self-blame and self-blame gives way to resentment, and resentment is where we would dwell all the days of our lives if it were not for a God who will not allow us to remain stuck if we are willing to seek Him.

So why did the older son stay, even after receiving twice what his younger brother got? The NIV Study Bible says, "The father might divide the inheritance but retain the income from it until his death." Perhaps the older son wanted that income and stayed to wait it out until his father's funeral. He could have been technically given his inheritance but might not have been allowed to keep anything he earned from it. In that case, it's entirely possible he remained out of resignation. Maybe a hollow duty truly was his only motivation. I can hear the older son: "I've done everything I was supposed to. I followed the rules. You didn't see it and you never offered me a banquet for doing everything correctly, for being the good child! Isn't there some reward for that?" I dearly love a footnote in *What's So Amazing About Grace?*, where Yancey writes of a preacher who modified the parable of the prodigal son for effect: "In a sermon, he had the father slip the ring and robe on the elder brother, then kill the fatted calf in honor of his years of faithfulness and obedience. A woman in the back of the sanctuary yelled out, 'That's the way it should have been written!'"[6]

Was the story of the lost son about those ungrateful Pharisees who weren't happy to see the prodigals come home? I read it as two stories. The traditional interpretation is obvious. But the gut-tightening indignation of the older brother is clearer to me than the world-weary resignation of the younger. I see this story as an example of Jesus' brilliant ability to speak to many and to one at the same time. It is a story that seeks to penetrate the traditions of an established institution as well as the walls of an individual heart.

As Jesus told the story of the prodigal son, the players were so obvious Jesus might have begun His tale with the opening from the old *Dragnet* radio and television series, "The story you are about to hear is true. Only the names have been changed to protect the innocent." I am sure the crowds delighted in the way He skewered the Pharisees. I can see them trying to locate in their peripheral vision the faces of any Pharisees in the throng to see the effect His accusations had on them. We love it when the high and-mighty are confronted with their hypocrisy, and the multitudes that followed Jesus weren't any different than we are.

But in the crowd might there have been an older son who felt again the sting of his parents' abandonment as he listened?

Parents can proclaim their love for the dutiful child . . . but then the lost one returns. They run to his side and care for him once again, preparing him for the next time he tells them he's leaving because he hates them. What kind of justice is that? What message is infused into a son's heart as he tries to figure out what God is like? By the time we are adults—we who are like the older son—the attempt to do everything perfectly to win the attention of the parents is so deeply imbedded in us we can't help our need to prove how intelligent we are, how capable we are, how self-sufficient we are, how much better we are than that worthless sibling to whom the parents give their all. For some of us, all we have is the resolve we've perfected to protect us from the pain of not being seen.

The truth is, though, we are seen by our heavenly Father. We may not always be seen in the ways that satisfy our human longings, but the formation of our character and the beauty of God's hand in our life circumstances are orchestrated with care, and we are recognized in a way we cannot see now. God knows what will shape us. It is not wrong to do things right, to demand that things be right. It is wrong, however, to assert our own righteousness. We don't have any of our own. Righteousness belongs to God, and in Jesus Christ, He gives us His.

Until we are set free from our need to perform, we will always insist on being seen for our righteousness instead of what He has given us. We will seek compliments and approval from as many others as we can gather to ourselves to try to fill that hole of desire for recognition from the parents. Many of us will become major achievers in our education or our careers. We may work to create the perfect family environment so we can write over the DVD of our childhoods. At any cost, we will show everyone how effortless it is to be "right," thus proving others are fools (our parents, our prodigal siblings). Out of every pore, we will exude the righteousness of the Pharisees, compelled to perform. When will we be able to do the same acts, but compelled only by joy and confidence that we are loved? "Having brought performance orientation to death, we may do exactly the same works, in much the same ways, but from an entirely different intent in the heart. In bringing performance orientation to death, we are not saying to stop serving and doing, but to die to the wrong hidden intents in the heart."[7] It's all about the "why" of what we're doing.

As Jesus tells His listeners that the father of His story said to his older son, "You have always been with me, and everything I have is yours," I feel the heart of the man in the crowd leap as he is touched with the possibility he may have missed the bigger picture of all that went on, of all that affected him. I feel that rush of illumination as he walks away, pondering the spark within him, not wanting to let it go, even though it might reveal something about himself he is reluctant to acknowledge, because there's truth in it, and he wants it, because he had heard Jesus say it would set him free.

— CHAPTER SIX —

Sitting by the Spring of My Injustices

The angel of the LORD found Hagar near a spring in the desert; it was the spring that is beside the road to Shur. And he said, "Hagar, servant of Sarai, where have you come from, and where are you going?"

—GENESIS 16:7-8

I can't remember thinking my childhood was anything seriously unusual. You would never have been able to convince me that I had experienced childhood trauma, not in the way that word is traditionally used, meaning an injury or an emotional shock. "Childhood trauma" immediately brings to mind something along the lines of abuse or neglect, but "trauma" itself has gradually taken on the definition of any kind of blow, sudden or sustained, immediate or collective. It is used clinically to describe various kinds of powerful events that can have a devastating effect upon people's views of themselves. One psychologist talks about "cumulative trauma,"[1] something that is assembled and saved up throughout our childhoods in our experiences with our parents. This may sound a bit sterile, but all it means is we have an ideal hope—normal childhood expectations—of our parents and families. We want them to be big and strong and always right, because that is what will protect us, and being part of them will make us big and strong, too, able to face what life presents to us. But when our ideal hope is repeatedly crushed by the truth of their behavior, by the evidence that our folks are not powerful or smart—perhaps they are obviously weak or passive, or criminal, or frightening—our frustrations, gathered over the years, have their own detrimental effect. We are hit with a double whammy: parents who aren't what we want them to be and the consistent disappointment of that fact.

To deal with this, we try to neutralize what we experience by making allowances for those we love. We may tell ourselves, "It's my fault that I expect so much." There is no one way kids react to the discovery of parental weakness, but there are common responses: a boy becomes angry and withdrawn and loses all confidence in and respect for his mom or dad. A girl creates a rich fantasy life through which she sees her parents as models of motherhood or fatherhood, and well into adulthood she defends her personal vision from all assaults of truth by other family members. Another child plays the role of the family mediator, struggling to be fair and view the situation practically, often twisting his or her loyalties into a pretzel in order to excuse and appease both sides.

So I didn't see what I was going through as trauma. It was my brother's trauma, or my mother's trauma, or my father's, but never mine. I wasn't involved. I wasn't there. I stayed out of it. I had a wonderful home life, I told people, and it was true in many ways. My parents loved me, I was not abused, I had a dog, I was allowed to have a phone in my room, I took piano lessons, my dad bought me a nifty little used car when I got my driver's license—what trauma did I experience?

I wouldn't say I denied what I experienced, either. I just didn't see it as having any lasting consequence. There were no physical bruises I could point to, no scars, no memories of being thrown out into the cold or denied food. In fact, I turned to food as an ultimate source of comfort. It was my own personal antidepressant, one with a serious side effect: I was always overweight, and along with having a wayward sibling in the house, this was one of the defining elements of my life. The self-loathing and depression that went hand in hand with my being heavy was temporarily mitigated every time I sat down to eat. And it was one of the few things that grabbed my parents' attention, even though it certainly wasn't the kind of attention I desired. It was painful beyond words to have my mother cluck disparagingly over my appearance and my father offer me money to lose weight. Mom's way of trying to shame me into dieting was to tell me that no boy would want to date me (true) and, later, no man would want to marry me (false) with my excess pounds. My woundedness at their disapproval of my looks, along with my outrage over their inadequate reactions to my brother's behavior, fueled a terrific defiance. I wrote them off. I loved them, but I ignored them almost completely, and kicked against nearly every parental stricture they attempted to enforce. It was my most potent form of protection—to pretend that I did not need them and to reject them before I received what felt like rejection. I covered over that aching hole I called my heart with layers of arrogance and disgust.

I was a Christian. I was a follower of the Lord Jesus Christ. Of all of the issues in my life, my attitude toward my parents was the gravest sin I've ever had to deal with. The guilt that would consume me after episodes of arguing was sickening. I would apologize to my mother, weeping in shame, wishing I could explain why I had so little control over my responses to her and Dad. Sometimes I tried, but I could not tell her the roots of my bitterness without accusing her. Her constant refrain to me was, "Why do you hate me?" She saw every response I made as a personal statement about her, when it was the whole family drama that filled me with distress. Compounding my dilemma was my conviction that I really didn't have a reason to be angry. I felt my rage was due solely to arrogance and pride I had to bring into submission to God. Every prayer I prayed began with a confession of my sins, the first being that I did not honor my father and my mother. Sure, I felt I was justified in my behavior— until I sat down to pray. That there might be other judgments attached to my temper, judgments concealed and unidentified that needed confession on their own, did not occur to me. I was just an evil, disgusting teenager. A *fat*, evil, disgusting teenager, filled with self-contempt.

This was my constant internal struggle: teeth-grinding anger followed by intense guilt. More than anything, I wanted to be able to rise above all that was boiling around me and be untouched by it, let it all go, allow the players to do what they wanted to do. Guilt dripped inside of me like a leaky faucet. Why couldn't I just let things be what they were?

I saw myself as a terrible daughter with a chip on her shoulder. Maybe if I'd received some teaching or counseling to help me pinpoint what was eating away at me, I could have brought it to the altar with insight. Instead, when I talked to adults about how angry I was at my mother, I got thoughtful but misguided speeches on mother-daughter relationships, because how could they have identified the offenses within me? Who could help me to see the roots of my bitterness so I could pray with words that would have helped me set them at the feet of Jesus? One motherly, older woman in the church whom I respected and in whom I had confided told my mother with a smile upon meeting her, "Why, I would have thought you'd be an ogre! I would have thought you'd have horns and a pitchfork the way your daughter talks about you!" You can imagine my shock when my mother related these flippant statements to me with choice words about her embarrassment. That was the last time I confided in that lady!

I could not see the source of my inner defiance at these confrontations as anything else but my own evil nature. Sometimes I held it in and paid my mother the penance of my regret, cleaning house and washing dishes to show her how contrite I was. Other times, I just gave in to the urge and fought back at her, telling her she didn't understand, she'd never understand, she made me crazy, she never listened to me. In all of this, my father was silent, perennially tired, retreating to his recliner in front of the television set, hoping to avoid all conflict. If he had created a personal motto, it would have been: "If I sit very, very still, nothing bad will happen."

When we first moved to California, a neighborhood family that befriended me with open arms used to call me by, as they put it, my "Indian name": Susan Morningstar. I think it may have been the name of a television cartoon character; I can't remember where it came from. Whenever I showed up at the door, my young friend or one of her brothers or her father would proclaim with delight, "Why, it's little Susan Morningstar!" Since then, I've added a few of my own "Indian names" that have been part of the roles forged for me or that I took on. The one most often used has been Girl With Strong Back, as in: "You're the strong one, honey." Oh, how I hated that name, then and well into my adult years. It meant my parents thought I didn't need anything. It meant I couldn't be weak. It meant that even if I didn't feel strong, I had to pretend to be strong, because everyone around me was falling apart. I hated it, but I used it, and tried to create an identity for myself in which I was above all that was going on, removed from its effects. I was smarter than what I saw around me. I was not going to fall into the whirlpool of extremes that beckoned day after day.

Another of my names was Little Susie Know Better. I convinced myself I had managed to remain untouched and had come out "normal." I had no desire to find a refuge in alcohol. The thought of being controlled by drugs was distasteful to me, and I was not interested in hanging around with people who thought drugs were cool. I saw people on drugs, or alcoholic acquaintances, as I saw my brother: witless, low-IQ losers. Their world was not mine. I wanted relationships, and it was very clear to me that alcohol and drugs did not create healthy ones.

Without a doubt, having committed my life to Jesus at an early age kept me from making terribly destructive choices, though I made my share of damaging ones. I wanted to be successful in life, and for me success meant contentment. I wanted real friendships, real choices, real joy, and I knew I needed to be clearheaded for these things. My roller coaster emotions were enough to deal with! The adolescent stuff I muddled through had to do with feeling inadequate, incapable, only mildly talented, less than perfect. Well into adulthood I often gave up instead of pursuing a dream or desire because I was sure I would never win it. I struggled with feelings of uselessness, alternating with some mysterious, subterranean belief I was made for great things. I knew I had gifts but I did not have the ambition to step out and use them. I feared rejection. I protected myself by making simple choices and taking the easier path when I came to a fork in the road.

I managed to get up every morning and get dressed and go to school, where I could be "myself"—outgoing and fun-loving. I adored school from the very first grade. My brain was a sponge: I stored facts and was challenged by tests and discovered history.

School was my refuge. There I was sincerely praised for my abilities and saw the smiles of my teachers when I surpassed their expectations. I was thrilled I had pleased them.

Going home, though, was a walk to the dungeon. Even now as I reflect on those years, I feel the heaviness that came over me with each step closer to my house. I methodically stripped myself of all of the day's accomplishments because there would be little acknowledgment there, other than a weary smile and a "That's good, honey," and a turning away to more pressing things. My parents said what they knew I wanted to hear but they could not know the sharp inner sensors of the child caught how forced the compliments often were. Even though I know now that my parents loved me and were proud of me, at the time I sensed by their manner that the attention they gave me was something they had to do so they could appease me and return to more urgent matters, such as my brother's latest problems.

The book of Genesis tells us of two women who each had a dream. One of them, Sarai, the wife of Abram, dreamed of having a son. The Lord had spoken to her and told her the dream would be fulfilled even though she was very old, far past the age of pregnancy. In that time and culture, bearing a child gave a woman identity. To be childless was a source of shame and yet Abram loved Sarai and apparently had never taken another wife, even though such an arrangement was common. Her identity was that of Abram's wife, but she longed for one as a mother.

The other woman, Hagar, Sarai's servant, dreamed of a place where she had significance, where she was important to someone. Hagar's situation existed because of a business arrangement. She and her service had been purchased. Here she was, tending to the needs of an old woman. Who would tend to hers when she got old? Her identity was that of Sarai's handmaiden while she longed to be a family member.

Both Sarai and Hagar tried to fulfill their dreams with what they had available to them. Even though God had told Sarai that she would have a son, she could not bring herself to believe that she, barren for many decades and now too old to make a baby, would actually give birth to the child herself. Could she hold on to the hope the Lord had given her that she would be able at last to fulfill the expectation of her culture and the deep desire of her heart? She could not. Even though she heard from the Lord of the Universe Himself, she still could not believe it. After a few years, she wondered if she'd heard at all.

"Perhaps," she may have thought to herself, "this is the way God meant that I would give Abram a son. I can give Hagar to him, since she is mine to give, and through her bear his child." Even though the Lord had been very specific with her about His plan, she decided to solve her problem on her own. She did not have the confident faith of her husband, who seemed to be able to simply listen and believe and follow no matter how unfathomable the instructions.

Hagar also had a plan. It was to make her dream a reality by inserting herself between Abram and Sarai. If a woman was unable to bear children, a son born by her husband to a servant would be raised as the heir, but it did not necessarily give the servant any right to consider herself a wife. She was a surrogate mother, always referred to in genealogies as "concubine." I sometimes wonder if Hagar suggested the arrangement to Sarai herself, knowing it was a common and socially acceptable practice. Here was her opportunity to be more than just a servant, a woman without a future or an identity; an attendant, acquired, like a rug or a bowl and with no more future than either. She could have children, and maybe that would be her ticket out of hopelessness. She knew she had no future without a husband and a child. She had no standing in life as someone's maid.

Genesis 16 says when Hagar knew she was pregnant, "she began to despise her mistress." Her plan seemed to be working. She could bear Abram a child; Sarai could not. Surely Abram would take her as his wife! She could supplant Sarai as the woman of the household. Her ability to have a child was nothing she could control, but owning this ability was the only card she had to play, and so she showed contempt for her mistress, who in turn had no control over her inability to have a child. Hagar thought she had made her dream come true, but eventually the situation deteriorated and Sarai blamed Abram for the mess of it all and resorted to mistreating Hagar. Unable to take it, Hagar escaped with her son.

What an injustice Hagar experienced! It was not Hagar's fault she was a servant, not her fault she had a fertile womb and became pregnant. On a human level, who could blame her for tossing her head and flaunting her big belly in triumph? Both women were guilty. Broken humanity is what God has dealt with since the time of Adam, and this culture had its cracks and fissures just as ours does today. Within every context God negotiates His plans, and with imperfect men and women He continues to accomplish His will. His purpose was for Sarai to bear a son of her own, but He did not reject Hagar for being a participant in the human attempts to do what only God could do.

Hagar ran away and found herself in the desert of abandonment and failure and rejection, sitting alone by a spring. There, the Bible tells us, God called to her and asked simply, "Where have you come from, and where are you going?"

God asks all of us, in one way or another, over and over throughout our lives, to tell Him where we have come from and where we are going. We most often hear the question deep inside when we are in positions of emotional injustice and pain. We want to answer with a strong defense, explaining to Him how hard we have worked, how misunderstood we have been. It's tough to admit where we have come from—a place of anger and resentment, a place of bitter observation of how little we are valued or how sadly impossible it is for those closest to us to communicate that we are cherished. Sometimes it is beyond our abilities to admit we may have helped place ourselves there with our own wrong motives and backfired strategies. Either way, our sinful retort is to throw up a shield and pull out all of our weaponry against those who have hurt us: revenge. A cold shoulder. Manipulation. Reminding offenders of past hurts; withholding love. Arrogance or victimhood. Can we be honest with God and tell Him truthfully where we have come from, instead of avoiding the question? We pad our answers with all kinds of unnecessary information, as though He can't figure out what we're talking about, as though He won't see the pain without our help.

God asked Hagar where she had been and where she was going, and she answered the first part, the easiest part for all of us. "I'm running away from my mistress," she told him. We all know where we have been and can, if given the opportunity, detail each step, index every road. For some of us, where we have been is a corner in our souls where we return to feel who we are, the space in our minds where we retreat to try to make sense of where we've ended up. Depending upon our circumstances, we find it a territory of comfort and favor or an oppressive state of constant replay. Our answer to God's first question places us for the second. So many of us are stuck wasting vital energy enumerating countless moments from our pasts, walking in a circle like a hiker lost in a forest. Others can't begin to explain where they've been because they can't believe there's any value in looking back. "What's past is past," they'll say, unwilling or unable to connect the dots of their early lives with their current ones to see the pattern that emerges.

God heard Hagar's complaint and did not reject it; after all, she was as honest as she could bring herself to be. She didn't sugarcoat her answer, didn't attempt to justify her actions. He left her an opening through which she could respond to His second question without demanding she answer it immediately. The Lord certainly knows how difficult we find it to see where our own choices are leading us. But He did not leave her without showing her He was present, that He was as engaged in her life as He was in Abram and Sarai's. As she sat by the spring, He spoke to her. "You are now with child and you will have a son. You shall name him Ishmael, for the LORD has heard of your misery" (Genesis 16:11). Ishmael means "God hears."

When we're brutally honest with ourselves and with God, when we can tell Him truthfully that, for instance, we are angry at the treatment we've experienced, we are far better off than those who cannot even begin to acknowledge their own sin and see how they came to be sitting by a spring in the desert after running away. But He doesn't want us to remain there. He hears us, He tells us where we are, reveals a little bit of His plan, and then expects us to take His gift and go somewhere with it, leaving behind the place where we wept for all that we had not received. He gives something to inspire. He provides us with the ability to submit to the lessons of life, forgive, and move on.

I have sat for long hours, over many days and years, by the spring of my injustices and felt its flow of miseries. I could not leave it: that spring lived within me and its flow ran down my cheeks whenever I thought of it. Until I understood I had a choice, I was ceaselessly spent and thirsty. I had a choice to name that spring. I could call it The Spring of Bitterness in my own Desert of Rejection. I could call it The Well of Discontent, the place where Girl With Strong Back drinks from The Water of Resentment and fuels herself with pain. Some of us shore ourselves up with the fire of our memories, using the heat to push us forward, and we know this is not always productive but we don't know how to put the fire out. How do we see the spring as sweet? How will we ever drink and be satisfied?

We must take the long road back, back to the place where we were mistreated, and live there until we receive word that all is accomplished. "Go back to your mistress and submit to her," said the Lord to Hagar. That submission comes with the promise that we will be blessed. It does not mean we will like it, that we relish the thought of return; it does not mean we forget what we have experienced. On the contrary, living with our remembrance is part of the cure, no matter how backwards it may seem. "Go back?" I can hear the exclamations.

"Go back to what? How do I do that?" Do I return to the center of the painful sore and just meditate on what it did to me? I've done that for years! What good will that do? Nicodemus said to Jesus, "Surely a man cannot enter a second time into his mother's womb to be born!" What value is there in being born again, he wanted to know. What good will it do to go back to the womb of our discontent and experience it all over again?

"Jesus answered, 'I tell you the truth, no one can enter the kingdom of God unless he is born of water and the Spirit. Flesh gives birth to flesh, but the Spirit gives birth to spirit. You should not be surprised at my saying, "You must be born again." The wind blows wherever it pleases. You hear its sound, but you cannot tell where it comes from or where it is going. So it is with everyone born of the Spirit' " (John 3:5-8).

We prodigal brothers return to our foundational springs for reasons that bring no refreshing. We go back when a word or an incident reminds us of every awful emotional upheaval: our siblings hit us up for money or make a scene in public or manipulate our parents. Our mothers or fathers continue to throw money at the situation or give us details about the family member we have no interest in hearing and then are perturbed with us because we don't sympathize. Family gatherings are heavy with unspoken questions and comments because it seems everyone prefers pretending. Once the adrenaline stops rushing through us like a flood, we sink down into memory and experience the sadness or rage that has grown up with us like a birthmark.

Years ago I heard a lecturer say that the only thing that will live after a nuclear holocaust will be roaches. They have systems, both physical and social, that cause them to resist nearly every adversarial force. It seems we'll never be rid of the disgusting creatures. With the same kind of morbidly fascinating indestructibility, our family scenarios are repeated decade after decade. Their power to survive is astounding, and even nuclear-force events cannot dislodge them. "I give up," we say to ourselves, but we really don't. We can't.

This is the power of flesh. It gives birth to its own. Sarai and Hagar's human-formed plans gave birth to a heap of relationship trouble. We're able to see this, and so we try to prevent re-creating the same old things with the power of flesh, but we are unsuccessful. We promise ourselves we will never give in, never submit, never again participate in the sick replaying of our childhood realities, but even if we have placed several states between ourselves and our families and refuse all communication, it only takes one letter, one phone call, to ignite the same old feelings of never having left. Since our resolutions don't hold, we attempt to find things that we think will distract us: we seek out certain kinds of relationships, flee to new locales, embrace behaviors and habits that give us temporary relief, and find we are confined to the deformed life they produce. Those roaches of past injuries hide in our dark places and breed. We can't do what needs to be done, Jesus told Nicodemus, by our own strength and determination.

No, it takes the power of the Spirit to put us where we need to be and be changed, made new, re-formed. We don't have the ability to place ourselves back in time and fix things or redo the past with a new understanding. But the Spirit of God has a way to transform our view. We can't understand how it works, but He does not require that we grasp the details. Once changed by the Spirit, the weight of the fixed place of emotional turmoil is eliminated. We become, figuratively, spiritually, "as light as a breeze." Wind rises up suddenly and is made known in the tallest branches of trees. You hear its effects, but you can't see the source of wind or determine its resting place. It has its own power. It's not fixed in the past or stuck in a particular moment. It touches one thing and everything. It can concentrate on specific regions or it can rest until its season calls it forth. That's how it is with everyone who's born of the Spirit, Jesus told us. We're not chained anymore to the sin and heartache that would define all of humanity. That is what Satan deeply desires: that we would be prisoners, slaves, not to physical events but to the more gripping turmoil and distress that resides in our emotional memories. Those who are born of the Spirit are free to move through the cracks of life's opposition and enter the caves of darkness and alert others to freedom.

Lots of things seem backward in the life of a Christian compared to our former way of life, where we depended upon a general idea of common sense. "Lose your life so that you can gain it," Jesus told His followers; "die so that you can live." His hearers found His concepts strange and confusing, and because we've heard them over and over we think we understand them. But put such opposite thinking into another context and we see how baffling it can be. In order to move forward, I must look back? In order to let go, I must hold on for a while? In order to be free, I have to *start over?*

Don't be surprised that you have to go back to the starting place. We prodigal brothers are still connected to our pasts by a cord that has been stretched so far in our attempts to escape it that it's as thin as fishing line, and as strong. We've convinced ourselves that if we get far enough away from our beginnings, either physically or emotionally, we will sever our affiliation with them. Not so. The cord needs to be cut at the origin, and then we can bid good-bye. Until then, the blood flows between our past and our present, grounding us in a place in time, never letting us forget that we are just servants to the events of our lives. There's a ceremony we must allow—a holy moment in our hearts that changes the view we have when we turn and look back. We thought the past meant one thing, and God shows us it meant another thing entirely.

The past exists, we cannot change it, it remains in place—but we can ascend like the wind and move to new places.

CHAPTER SEVEN

First We Must Grieve

It is not that parents are to blame. Whatever parents were, saints or hellions, normal people or psychos, what is important is the child's reactions. . . . In every way we have reacted sinfully, we have set in motion forces that must be reaped, unless mercy prevails. We do not blame parents by seeing that the root and trunk of all life is formed with them. . . . In dealing with the normal sinfulness of us all, blame is not part of the game, totally irrelevant like a player who never got into the ballpark, much less up to bat. All of us have been born with sinful hearts into a sinful world.

—JOHN AND PAULA SANDFORD[1]

I am drawn to people who have lived a long time and their fascinating life stories. A woman I used to visit in a nursing home told me of coming to California in a covered wagon. Another talked to me about tending the chickens on a farm in an area of Los Angeles now so populated I couldn't begin to imagine open land there. Still another relived her preparations for dances: putting on her dress with the bright red sash and smiling at how exciting it was to have young men ask to sign her dance card.

My love of hearing the life experiences of those born long before me was reinforced when I did my clinical psychology internship in a senior center. I was told of growing up in the 1930s in New York City, of waiting for the train that was bringing a loved one home after service in World War II, of joyous love affairs, thoughtless children, and fortunes gained and lost. One of my jobs was to facilitate a couple of small groups for those dealing with grief. Usually the grief was for the loss of a spouse; sometimes it was the loss of an adult child. The strain that most of the participants felt with expressing the pain they were going through was heartrending. Part of it was the conventions of their generation: one did not air one's personal laundry for others to evaluate. Grief is a private matter, one of them might say, embarrassed to open up in front of a small gathering. Yes, I'd respond, and this is a private group. It's just for people who are grieving, not for the rest of the world to hear.

One by one, they would let out some of their anguish and sorrow. They would talk of their spouses and how they didn't know how to walk through life without them. They would relate memories, not always happy ones. Even those who had difficult marriages with troublesome husbands or wives told of how lonely they were.

"Why do I need to do this?" one man barked at me. I told him he was under no obligation to attend the group. He had come on his own. "My kids keep telling me I need to deal with my grief," he snarled. "I don't think I should spend time dwelling on it. My wife is gone, and there's nothing I can do about it." In spite of his words, we all felt the undercurrent of his suffering. One woman responded softly, "You can't push it away. You have to acknowledge that she lived and you miss her. Not thinking about her says she's not worth remembering."

A sob broke from the man's throat, and there were tears in the eyes of several in the group as we waited for him to compose himself. He managed to make some comments about what a good mother she had been to their children. But he did not return to the group the following week. Talking about her made him feel worse, and holding all of his memories at arm's length was the only way he knew to protect himself from overwhelming feelings. He could not know that after a while, talking about her would give him a release from those emotions and allow him, someday, to remember his wife with less pain and more pleasure at the good memories.

The way one "deals" with grief is to fall into it and feel it right down to the toes of its existence. Grief has to overtake us, to wrack us with the agonies of aloneness and emptiness and loss. Therapists have coined a term for helping those in bereavement: "grief work." The fact is that grief *is* work. It is there in the morning when we wake up, rides us all day, and lies down with us at night, even entering our dreams and leaving its footprints all over our emotions. With most people, grief will have its course, different with each person, but it will wash a man or woman ashore eventually. The time will come when one has truly bid the last good-bye, after giving the person's memory a special place in the heart to remain forever. Life will begin to return to something resembling normal, and one will feel the sunlight after the long cloud of bereavement has passed over.

Throughout my life, I alternated between a little bit of understanding and a lot of vexation over the state of affairs between my brother and my parents. Into adulthood, as my perspective was pried open enabling me to see some of the deeper consequences of my growing-up years and the relationships I had with each member of my family, I began to understand the foundations of my fierce bitterness. I came to see from where it all flowed, but I couldn't plug the source to keep it from wounding me again and again. It had a hold on me. Whenever I would talk about the events of my youth and would confess my loathing and sorrow for all of it, someone would invariably get that I-feel-your-pain look on his or her face and say, "You have to let it go."

That statement usually sent me right to the moon. *Let it go! How do I let it go?* I was told I needed to, but never told how to do it. I *couldn't* let it go. I wasn't holding on to it; *it* was attached to *me*! I couldn't find the cord that bound the thing to me so that I could cut it. I was sick of it—sick of my hard feelings, sick of my conceit, sick of the despair that came rushing up from the well inside after talking with my mom or dad and hearing that they were continuing to sacrifice their wills, their money, their health, and their sanity to my brother. Could anyone ever tell me *how* to "let it go"?

After a time, I could articulate the pain and sadness I had grown up with, the hostility I directed at my brother, and the pity I felt for my parents. But I couldn't see a way to let it go other than to just keep praying—another one of those well-meaning platitudes I was offered—so why keep working at it? So much of my early Christian instruction had been that one should avoid negative thoughts, reject and actually rebuke them, because to focus on them was a complete lack of spiritual maturity. Spiritually mature people focus only on the good, the perfect, whatever is noble, whatever is pure. There was nothing more negative for me than dipping a finger in the pool of my memory and holding on to the emotions disturbed by my touch.

But that is precisely what I needed to do. I needed to sit with the memories of my injuries and hold on to them, not in the same adhesive way in which they bound themselves to me, but hold on to them and acknowledge their existence. My experiences and the feelings attached to them are a massive contributor to the person I have become, to all that I am, and I spent a lifetime ultimately dismissing their importance.

Like the gentleman whose children urged him to address his loss, I could not understand the value of laying out my feelings and examining them. If anything, I thought I examined them too much. I was an expert at my own psychoanalysis. If you'd asked, I could have told you much more than you wanted to hear.

Those like me have come to hate that forest of hurt in which we keep running around the same huge tree, discovering with shock that we haven't traveled far at all. Yet it's in that place that we must stop and carefully observe our surroundings. We need to be quiet. We need to listen to the sound of wind in trees and branches and leaves. The wind moves unseen through every aspect of our lives, but we're so eager to be rid of what irritates us we can't hear the song made by its movement. We have to listen to what's grown inside of us, what has branched out, what has taken deep root.

Physical death is not the only loss that produces grief. Some of us have lost time. We have lost normal human expectations. We have lost relationships. We have lost love, or innocence, or faith in someone or something we trusted, such as our ability to control circumstances. Maybe we have lost a childhood, or were stuck negotiating the twists and turns of life without one or both parents, or we missed the feeling of ever being in good health, and we are bruised again every time we think of it. These things need to be grieved, too. We can't change anything about them, but the loss is there and demands our attention. Not to acknowledge it means it wasn't worth remembering.

I did acknowledge it, but I had never moved on past acknowledgment to grieve the deep loss I felt over missing out on a drug-free, alcohol-free, insanity-free, chaos-free family. I had never grieved that I could not find peace in my home. I had not allowed the grief that my parents had little left to give to me after they'd spent all of their emotional resources on my brother. Grief is not judgment about right or wrong. Grief is not blame. It is simply the anguish of loss. I needed to mourn the loss of those missing pieces, embracing them and then bidding them goodbye, finding a place in my heart for them to dwell in memoriam.

I finally saw that if I didn't mourn and release my past, I would repeat it simply by playing it over and over and over, running it like an annoying song stuck in my thoughts, dealing with those repeated frustrations in memories that never let me go, no matter how free and successful and transcendent appears my present life.

God calls us to deeper tasks. We must look upon our sin, our pain, our tragedy, our regret. We have to humble ourselves and acknowledge it all completely before we can release it. The Sandfords say, "To be transformed *by* the renewal of the mind does not mean that we must all become auto-analysts, excavating every moment of our history into the light (or confusion) of mental awareness. Some things may be better left unseen and unsaid. Sometimes the Lord renews our deep mind without our ever having consciously understood. We simply find ourselves thinking differently. . . . If the *heart* is changed by the Lord, the mind, both conscious and subconscious, is *renewed*. Sometimes we simply grow out of a childish way. We have thought as children and reasoned so, but when we became adults in Christ, we put that away (1 Corinthians 13:11)."[2]

But what's gone on in my life is a lot more than just a child's way of reasoning. How shall I be transformed? I learn from the story of Hagar and the questions put to her in the desert, and the admonishment that she had to return to the source of her unhappiness so that God could bless her. I have to believe it has a benefit because the Lord Himself gave the instruction.

We can, in a perverse way, camp around our hurt and anger because it is comfortable. We keep wanting a resolution, a reason, an apology—what we are fond of referring to as *closure*. It's an impossible expectation. The fact is we will never receive what it is we want to receive. We can't go back and become that long-gone child and get what we want and need. We must be watchful of the possibility of making an altar to that grief and lying upon it, waiting for what will never come.

Not mourning my losses and experiencing the insight that comes only from that walk is like not burying a loved one who dies. There's no life left in the body, but I don't want to face the burial. I'm afraid if I don't have the body, I will forget what it was like to have the person with me, so I must keep it close by, even if artificially. For some of us, our pain defines us, lets us know we're alive, keeps us from feeling completely alone. We may not have anyone else, but we'll always have our pain. The truth is that in grief, a part of us dies, and like a seed that part must die before it can begin to grow.

The Sandfords speak of going through Gethsemane, where we acknowledge our pain and trepidation before the Father and trustfully keep going. It's there we weep out our sadness and apprehension, "until it is no longer important whether we or the other guy is right or wrong. . . . Our visit to Gethsemane is not complete so long as we are still marshaling our defenses of our rightness and cataloging the other's sins."[3]

Most people have seen the famous painting of Jesus in Gethsemane, looking like some Hollywood film star of the 1940s with flowing brown locks draped across his shoulders. Positioned before a rock with his hands folded, his face is turned upward into a light that bathes his kneeling figure. But Gethsemane was not lovely. It was not beautifully combed hair and a neatly trimmed beard. It was not clean clothes and soft light. It was a place of internal confrontation with the reason Jesus was born. It was there He said, "Not what I want, but what You've decided is most important." It was there He sweat drops of blood as He prayed, "If it is possible, let this cup pass from me." He knew what was coming. He was as much man as He was God, and the man knew that a ghastly, horrific death was approaching. On a human level, even when you know that something you have to go through is necessary and you're willing to do it, the fear can be gripping.

Did He review His years in Nazareth? Did He think about the lavish gifts that were brought to Him by wealthy foreigners when He was a child, gifts His mother may have kept and surely spoke of many times? Did He remember Joseph, the one who had raised Him, and what His earthly mother and father had gone through to ensure His passage to this very day? Maybe He saw the faces of all of His dearest friends, recalled the joy of days spent exploring and nights given over to stories, to debate, to sharing. Perhaps He mentally walked with His mother once again to the market, remembering conversations, moved by her love for Him. The deep relationships He had formed with each of His disciples, the hunger for the kingdom of God He saw in their eyes . . . He was about to leave all of these things behind, and even though He was willing to go, the journey was not simple or easy. He would have to let go of all that had defined Him in His walk as the Son of Man.

In my own Gethsemane, I review the many scenes of disappointment. I have to let go of all of those awful judgments that have defined me; the badges of personal goodness, the view of myself as right and everyone else as wrong. I know I have to lay it down. It's necessary. But it requires grieving before I go.

It's time for my own burial: "The moment the attitude of our hearts finds its death knell on the cross, the structures it sustained begin to find their death on the cross. . . . Like Jesus, after a while (three days and three nights in the belly of the earth), a new and resurrected spirit in us fills that old, newly dead structure with a new and transformed intention."[4] The only way to be born again is to die and be born of the Spirit. To be released I have to die to the past to which I am bound.

C. S. Lewis's book *A Grief Observed* was compiled from a journal he kept after his wife's devastating death. They had been married only a short while when she died; in fact, they had married knowing that she had cancer and would not survive long. After a long, dark period of deep despair and doubt, he began to make tiny steps toward the light of day. Referring to his wife as "H." throughout the journal, he writes:

Something quite unexpected has happened. It came this morning early. For various reasons, not in themselves at all mysterious, my heart was lighter than it had been for many weeks. . . . And suddenly at the very moment when, so far, I mourned H. least, I remembered her best. Indeed it was something (almost) better than memory; an instantaneous, unanswerable impression. To say it was like a meeting would be going too far. Yet there was that in it which tempts one to use those words. It was as if the lifting of the sorrow removed a barrier. Why has no one told me these things? How easily I might have misjudged another man in the same situation? I might have said, "He's got over it. He's forgotten his wife," when the truth was, "He remembers her better because he has partly got over it."[5]

Once we have cut that cord that bound us to our experiences, we are born anew in remembering. We can remember with more clarity and greater understanding when we've done the distressing work of grieving. Remembering my past these days does not bring on the depression it once did. The lifting of sorrow removes the barrier that prevents me from seeing God's hand even in the most devastating of circumstances, and gives me the power to appreciate how the Lord knew what would construct this building named Sue. "Perhaps we can learn nothing more valuable in all of life than to trust that He really is who He is, and will accomplish what He has purposed to do."[6]

That is where I come from. Shall I sit near a spring in the desert and hold on to my bitterness and gall? Shall I forever seek someone to tell me they love me just for who I am, that they like me, that they think I am a wonderful person, that I bring something to life? "Where have you been?" has been answered. But the opportunity to provide the details of the past has come to an end. Now I must answer the second question: "Where are you going?"

What we have to concede is the answer can honestly be, "I am not going anywhere." I can choose to lie by the spring like the man who waited at the pool of Bethesda for years on end. This pool had healing properties and it was thought that an angel occasionally whipped through the pool, and when the people saw the waters churning and immediately went in, they were cured. "When Jesus saw him lying there and learned that he had been in this condition for a long time, he asked him, 'Do you want to get well?' " (John 5:6). I have thought about this man hearing the question and thinking to himself, "What are you—*crazy*? Why do you think I've been lying by this pool all these years, waiting for the angel to stir the waters? Of course I want to get well! It's not my fault I have no one to help me!" But Jesus' question ignored the obvious, which so easily fools the eye, and looked for the invisible: desire and intention. If the man had truly wanted to get well, he would have figured out a way to get into that water when it was agitated. Sometimes we want others to *think* we want to get well when we really just want to lie on our mats by Bethesda and forever lament our pain.

The time comes when the grievance has been registered. God has heard. He then gives us direction to move on. There comes a time when deep inside I hear a voice saying, "Stop grieving now."

It is time for me to name the spring. Genesis 16:13 says of Hagar, "She gave this name to the LORD who spoke to her: 'You are the God who sees me,' for she said, 'I have now seen the One who sees me.' " The spring by which she sat became known as Beer Lahai Roi, which means "well of the Living One who sees me." I can imagine her taking Ishmael to this well many times as he grew up, explaining to him this was the place where God told her what he should be named and what his character would be. I can imagine every time she went to that well, she remembered she had been asked, "Where have you come from, and where are you going?" I can imagine each time she attended that well, she thought of how far she had come from a difficult and lonely situation.

Today my Indian name means something vastly different. "Girl With Strong Back" was a name I resented. Today I know that God gave me this name. My strength was not my own work, but His. He put me in a place where my strength could provide something, where He could use the characteristic He had planted within me, where the call He had placed upon me would be moved to action. I had wanted to do great and mighty things for God, work for Him in some marvelous capacity that rang loudly and lit up like a slot machine. That would be just the ticket, I thought: I can be used by God, and everyone will see it! The great and mighty thing, however, was the attribute I scorned, the feature I despised because it was used in obscurity: my strength. He had placed it and wanted to use it, and use it He did. How wonderful it would have been if I could have seen it then! I could have received real joy in knowing I was doing what I was meant to do. Nevertheless, by His grace and immeasurable wisdom, He used what He had given me for the people who needed it.

Girl With Strong Back finally understood she carried much *because she could.* Hagar comprehended that the God of her master and mistress wasn't blind to her. He didn't see Abram and Sarai exclusively. "You are the God Who Sees *Me*" was Hagar's new perspective, and it gave her the energy to return and face all she had been up until that point so she could be something different from now on: a woman with an identity. That identity might not be seen by anyone else, but she now knew it was recognized by the Lord God Almighty, and if He sees it, who else is necessary? The past was not gone, but because it was returned to, submitted to, and embraced for the part it had to play, it became the lens through which she saw her new self, the one God had created.

The Lord made Hagar the mother of a nation of people. "His hand will be against everyone and everyone's hand against him," God told her, "and he will live in hostility toward all his brothers." Just because we are given a revelation that changes our approach to life does not mean everyone we touch will be similarly transformed. The outside world may not change at all. It may even grow worse. But we have been to the desert and back, and our responses are no longer captive to our immaturity. Our immaturity had us focusing on ourselves, when God wants to influence other people's lives. That immaturity is our sinful reaction to His will, and we can now see it for what it is, confess it, and travel on. We know the most important questions: "Where have you been, and where are you going?" Each time they are asked, we should be able to answer with greater clarity and truthfulness.

Chapter Eight

If You Don't Love, You Don't Know

I have to let go of all comparison, all rivalry and competition, and surrender to the Father's love. This requires a leap of faith because I have little experience of non-comparing love and do not know the healing power of such a love. As long as I stay outside in the darkness, I can only remain in the resentful complaint that results from my comparisons. Outside of the light, my younger brother seems to be more loved by the Father than I; in fact, outside of the light, I cannot even see him as my own brother.

—HENRI NOUWEN[1]

My mother left a number of cassette tapes of Bible studies she conducted and talks she gave at women's meetings. Mom believed that my brother was the result of his genetic heritage—not organically, but spiritually, and during one talk she presented her conviction that demonic powers follow family lines. These demons can be diseases or habits, physical conditions or character traits. "Parents, you need to bind these demonic forces over your children," she said, and illustrated the way she prayed for my brother, breaking the power of what she insisted were generational laws that had to be specifically addressed.

"Let me tell you about my son," she said. "He's always been trouble. Defiant. Rebellious. Hardheaded." She talked about how she and my father did not realize he was on drugs. She related examples of his behavior, his violent threats, how frightening he could be.

"Our daughter told us we needed to put him out. Many times, she would say, 'Mom and Dad, kick him out! Put him out on the street! Let him hit rock bottom and have nowhere else to turn, because then he'll have to turn around.' My husband and I thought about that, but it just didn't sit right in our spirits. We prayed about it, and we decided that wasn't the way we were going to handle it." She went on to insist my brother was responding to her prayers, that he was making progress, and she simply had to remain diligent to pray against these demons of generational influence.

I listen to those old tapes from the dimension where the future has taken place, and I know what is coming: many more years of heartache, defiance, rebellion, violence, and threats. I don't necessarily doubt my mother's theories. They weren't hers, really, but ideas she came across that appealed to her. But I know that in this case they had no practical effectiveness.

I listen from the shadow, and I know she and my father never got to see him as she so confidently claimed my brother would be and, in fact, just 20 years into the future both my mother and my brother would be gone.

The parable of the prodigal son departs from my experience in the portrayal of the compassionate father, not because my parents were not compassionate, but because their compassion was expressed in imprudent ways. Jesus obviously wanted to explain what God is like, and my history made this difficult to see. Nevertheless, I relate so much to the parable because He describes my heart clearly in the words of the older brother and shows me the feelings God has for me. The father went to the older son. He didn't leave this part of the story hanging. Was this story simply a giant hint to the Pharisees who listened in order to find fault? Was it a story of how the Lord searches for us? Was it the story of a family? It's all of these things, and more. I don't suggest we discard the obvious metaphor Jesus used for a loving heavenly Father, but there is so much to be seen in the parable it's like unpacking boxes that have been in storage: "Oh, I forgot I had this!" we proclaim as we unwrap some treasure, and it feels like we received a gift. There are fresh ways to see old things, and God provides the vision.

While my parents were preoccupied with my brother's problems, this did not make me any less their child, and the father's preoccupation in the story with the younger son does not make the older son a worthless character. For me, the older son is not just a device Jesus used to pinch the listening Pharisees. The father loved him, too. He didn't tell him to drop dead or to straighten up and fly right. He demonstrated clearly in the parable that the father loved the older son, and this is what I need to hear. He loves me. I, too, am the apple of His eye. He does not want me to stand out in the cold, but will come and plead for me to stay on track with Him. As long as I am following Him, there is a purpose to all that occurs. The Word tells us *in all things* He is working (Romans 8:28). He may not have caused the things; we may have done that for ourselves, or others may have treated us poorly. But He works on those hard things, slowly bringing them to the surface, polishing them up, and revealing them to be gems that can transform our outlook and behavior.

The Apostle Paul admonished us to "rejoice in our sufferings, because we know that suffering produces perseverance; perseverance, character; and character, hope" (Romans 5:3-4). We're usually willing to admit that suffering produces character, but we don't want to accept the character-building nature of our pain when we're going through it. It's—well, *painful*, and how many times have we cried out when hurting, "Is this really helping me, Lord? Is this supposed to be good for me?" I certainly could not see what was being built in me as I suffered through never-ending episodes of intense family drama. Like Job, I would groan at God: "Does it please you to oppress me?" (Job 10:3). But, also like Job, I could not see what was going on behind the scenes in the heavenly Situation Room. Job had no way of knowing he had been challenged before God Almighty with the assertion that he was devoted to the Lord only because of his prosperity. "His commitment is skin deep," Satan told the Lord. "Take what you've given him and he'll curse you!"

So Satan was given permission to unload upon Job a wheelbarrow full of the awful effects of life on this earth: the death of his children in a tornado, the loss of his livelihood by marauders and fire, a horrible affliction upon his body. Job did not know that God had not killed his children or burned his sheep, nor could he know that God's confidence in his character was being contested by the rebellious angel who hated anything the Father loved. That confidence was immediately satisfied when Job "fell to the ground in worship and said: 'Naked I came from my mother's womb, and naked I will depart. The LORD gave and the LORD has taken away; may the name of the LORD be praised' " (Job 1:20-21). The next verse tells us plainly Job did not sin in saying this. He did not wrongly accuse God; he spoke what he believed in his heart.

"Of course, Job had no inkling of the discussion going on in heaven between God and Satan," wrote Brent Curtis and John

Eldredge. "It was a debate over whether the foundation of God's kingdom was based on genuine love or power. And astonishingly, God was placing the perception of his own integrity as well as the reputation of his whole kingdom on the genuineness of Job's heart."[2] That Job professed God had a right to do with him as He pleased and praised the name of the Lord for it in the midst of such terrific calamity says volumes about Job's character.

Many people in the same situation would decide there was no worth in knowing God, no point in worshiping a Being who would allow tremendous suffering, and would end their relationship with Him. For a lot of folks, it doesn't take losing children or money or houses to curse God. I've known people who have told me plainly if God allowed their abusive father or a convicted criminal or a particular psychopathic dictator into heaven, they'd curse God. The world does not understand, and many Christians do not even grasp, that Satan is a force in this world and has a power to inflict horrific suffering and pain while we are here. The adversary has authority that God is permitting for a time. But that time will come to an end because a righteous legal process was set into motion with the birth, death, and resurrection of Jesus Christ. Until then, Satan, who despises us because we are the cherished treasures of the Master of the Universe, works to destroy us.

Job didn't know Satan was behind his suffering. In his extreme adversity he complained, he railed, he defended his actions and demanded that God speak to him and tell him what he'd done wrong. As his friends listened, they took his lament as evidence of sin, because he couldn't figure out where he had failed to please God. "Admit it!" they pressed him. "You had to have done something wrong! No one suffers without a reason!" They were right—suffering is not without reason, but it wasn't at all what they insisted it was. Yet Job never wrongly accused God, although he came pretty close! He wept out his frustration and torment pleading for vindication, but he never turned away from God.

Today, in the new covenant, we are told plainly about our adversary. We are urged to resist him and told what weapons we must use to defeat him. We are educated in the ways of our enemy and the strategies we're to employ. Jesus told us about his character—"he was a murderer from the beginning . . . a liar and the father of lies"—and the intent of such a criminal: "to steal and kill and destroy" (John 8:44, 10:10). We have insight Job did not have. We know the Evil One's desire is to put us out of the race, to thwart every good thing that God would accomplish.

But we have Job's example in his unwillingness to let go of God in the midst of crushing physical and emotional agony, when holding on seemed futile and maybe even harmful. For me, the story of Job is not about standing patiently under the afflicting hand of God. God permitted what Job experienced but He was not the afflicter. And not every awful thing that happens to us is from the devil; we do a lot of things to ourselves without any help from an evil power. The Bible promises to give us discernment so we might wage our battles with the proper weapons, and tells us that with maturity, we will train our senses to be attuned to evil (Hebrews 5:14).

But whether we are facing demonic trials or dealing with the consequences of our own or another's poor choices, or we're simply dealing with the effect of sin upon the human race, I learn from Job not to let go. I am to trust God will fulfill His plans and purposes for me. God really is sovereign. I don't get to dictate to the Lord what must and must not happen to me. As His child, I have His Word and I come to Him with reminders of His promises. I am confident His plans for me are for my good, "plans to prosper you and not to harm you, plans to give you hope and a future" (Jeremiah 29:11).

Sometimes it's hard to see how His plans prosper me! But I must humble myself and express with Job, "The Lord has the right to give and to take away, and I will bless His name in all circumstances." Because His plans for me are always good, always loving, somehow the Lord will make circumstances ultimately work in my favor, if for nothing more than revealing in me the very things He wants to root out. Oswald Chambers posed a question he knew his Bible college students were asking, and then gave them an answer: " 'Is this a God of mercy, and love?' you say. Seen from God's side, it is a glorious ministry of love. God is going to bring you out pure and spotless and undefiled; but He wants you to recognize the disposition you were showing—the disposition of your right to yourself."[3] Job didn't hold on to any of his possessions—his health and personal happiness, his children, or his home—as though he deserved them. He viewed them as privileges handed to him by the Lord.

What made Job blameless and upright was even as he endured heartbreaking loss and devastating physical ailments and wept with the memory of the good that had been his, he did not reject the God he knew in his heart was his Provider and Redeemer. How many times when we are in the midst of suffering do we want to flee, to run from the relationship we think is *causing* our pain, instead of finding a way to hold on to El Shaddai and express to Him every thought, no matter how self-incriminating?

God did not whack Job for complaining. What He did was very emphatically correct Job for suggesting He was indifferent, responding to Job's soliloquies with a big fat reminder of who is really in charge. He spoke to Job as honestly as He'd been spoken to, with the same vigor and even the same sarcasm! "So, you know My purpose in every single thing that goes on in this world, and you're going to tell me how I should execute my plans," God said. "You know when the deer give birth and you help them in their labor because of your great compassion. Oh, and *you* gave the wild donkey a place to play because you delight in its personality. And, oh yes, I see it now—*you* gave the horse its strength and take pride in its fearlessness, because you created everything and you know the significance of every creation, of every activity, of every moment in every event!" Job admitted he had no way of knowing the inside scoop. "I spoke out of my ignorance," he confessed.

In the end, God saw His purpose with Job fulfilled and blessed him more richly than before, telling Job's friends, "You have not spoken of me what is right, as my servant Job has" (42:8). Job may have taken his complaining to the outer edges, but his protests acknowledged God always had the final word. Maybe Job never found out what had gone on in the council of heaven, how truly significant his commitment had been; he just did the best he could with the limited knowledge he had. He kept hanging on to The One Who Sees Me, and that pleased God.

I remember begging my mother to kick my brother out. I wanted my suffering alleviated. That it would eventually produce something I could not have imagined was impossible to foresee. God fulfilled His plans with me in this family, even though, like Job, I thought God didn't care about what was happening. I wanted my mother's and my father's travails to end. I wanted Him to fix things *my* way, by fixing my parents or my brother. But the Lord did not create my family to live in agony just so I would have some rock-solid character. It's just that there's a time when we are urged to recognize what we are going through is so much bigger than we are that we need to go with the flow and let it have its ultimate effect. It's only when we've been tested that we know what we're made of and what the Lord provided for us so we could make it through the trial. That's what faith is: the trust that the Father will do in us what He said He would do. He'll fulfill His promises, oh yes! The thing hard to embrace is He'll always do it the way *He* wants to do it.

"Anyone who does not love his brother, whom he has seen," wrote John, "cannot love God, whom he has not seen" (1 John 4:20). Here is the barometer of my relationship with God: in direct proportion to my ability to love my brother is my capacity to love the Lord. If I cannot love my parents in spite of their flaws and failures, I am severely limited in my relationship to the Father. If I cannot love my brother even though he was damaged, irritating, sinful, lacking conscience, but I say I love the Lord, who am I kidding? Certainly not God! I don't want to love my brother. He didn't earn it. I don't want to display forgiveness for my parents. They didn't ask for it. Their hearts may reach out for my love; God sees and asks me to do His bidding though I don't have the evidence I require. But I don't want to love, and there is the picture of my relationship to God. Can we not love those closest to us? Then we do not love God.

"God has poured out his love into our hearts by the Holy Spirit, whom he has given us" (Romans 5:5). The King James Version says, "The love of God has been shed abroad in our hearts." I used to own two gorgeous ex-racing Greyhounds, and I know about shedding! In spite of assurances by adoption group representatives that Greyhounds do not shed as much as other dogs, my two discharged enough hair every other day to clothe another dog. "Abroad" was the old English term to denote covering a large area. "Shed abroad" has significance for me. It's not that we don't have the love to give; it's that we don't have to work up our own love to do the right thing. The Lord is shedding His own quality of love onto us so that we can gather it and put it to use.

I found insight into this principle decades ago by the late John Osteen in a little booklet he wrote called *The Divine Flow*. It is simple but penetrating, and has given me a keen awareness of the reality of the presence of the Holy Spirit in my life. Jesus was moved with compassion, and that compassion went out to people, and He always followed it, Osteen explained. When He did, things happened! That same compassionate love of the Lord Jesus can rise in our hearts at times we least expect it, and we must learn to follow that flow of love. We don't have to work it up. "Just stay full of love and pray," he wrote. "Stay full of the Holy Ghost. . . . Then when you feel God's love flowing through you to a certain person, act right then."[4]

My own love may have dried up, but the love of Jesus is a never-ending fountain! I may not be able to become an entirely different person to those who have given me grief, but I can follow the divine flow when it activates and do things, say things, *be* something I would never have been able to be on my own, and it's these sporadic instances of kindness and compassion that will do worlds more than all of the fake, gritting-my-teeth-pretending-to-love-you performance could ever do. God's Word, impelled by God's Spirit, which expresses itself in love and is shed abroad in our hearts, will accomplish something far greater than our measly little efforts to "be loving." If we let Him lead us and follow that flow of love when it surfaces, God can intensify its effects and cause it to speak to the other person in a profound way. It might be nothing more than the sudden desire to call and ask how things are going, or feeling compelled to buy a little gift or take someone to lunch. It just might be something huge, something we wouldn't normally do—but then, if we are actually feeling true compassion and love for those who have seriously hurt us, that's not something we would normally do either, is it? Must be God.

There *is* something going on we cannot see, and learning to walk with God in the midst of fires and earthquakes and floods and floggings may not be our idea of good training, but who are *we* to say we know ourselves better than the Potter? We're the clay! We can't say to Him, "Hey, I want a nice curve in the artwork right here, and carve off that excess." Do we honestly think we can *see ourselves* as we spin upon that wheel? And would we really have the courage to instruct Him to trim the excess that isn't beneficial? We don't even know what He's creating, so how can we know what doesn't belong in the finished product? Our direction to Him would most certainly produce a shapeless mess. Sometimes it can feel like He's thrown us in the kiln before He's finished molding us, but it's really just the friction of His hands upon our flesh. We've got to be willing to remain upon that altar. What we're going through may not be for us, but for someone else. We don't always get to know. These days when I sense I'm being perfected by the Artist of my soul, I reassure myself with, "This will be *great* testimony material when it's all over."

Brennan Manning said that people "come to us hungry for understanding, thirsting for affirmation, naked with loneliness and wanting to be covered with the mantle of our genuine concern. So often I refuse to give it to them. I'm not really interested in their hopes, fears, dreams, joys, aspirations and disappointments. Yet I claim that I am dedicated to God, that I live for Jesus Christ, that I am dedicated to my religion. What kind of religion is this?"[5]

How should I have loved my brother? I still don't know. It's hard to imagine how I might have loved him rightly because I was not mature enough to understand the complexities of love. There is love in discipline. There is love in an expectation demanded and held to for a person's good. It wasn't my job, though, to discipline him, and the expectations I established as an adult were negative: I expected him to lie, I expected him to act hatefully, I expected him to always disappoint. I don't know what actively loving him would have looked like. If I had it to live over, knowing what I know now . . . I might still struggle with how to love him, but I would at least be clear on why it is necessary. I wouldn't give him money, but I could have listened sometimes instead of just hanging up the moment I heard his voice. I'm sure Jesus listened to a whole lot of worthless talk from some of the rabble He hung out with.

Today my challenge is different, presenting itself in new ways. I cared for my father as his mind deteriorated, and I'd ask myself: *How can I love him?* With all I know, with all that has transpired, how can I love this man over whom I have made such strong judgments? My answer: by forgiving him for not being more than he is. By recognizing that some things may never be resolved in this lifetime, and my desire for a wonderful relationship with him is probably one of them. I can hold on to knowing if he never did another right thing as long as he lived, he did this: he saw an abandoned baby in a bassinette and gave his heart away, determined to make her his own child. Whatever bad he did and good he left undone, I could still honor that act that gave me a future and a hope. The love of God shed abroad in my heart, the divine flow, rose up within me and showed me his fragility, his meager ability to put two and two together, his faulty reasoning, and I could find tenderness for his weakness.

As I see it, there's even more evidence scripturally to warn me of my need to love my parents by forgiving them and releasing my resentments. Proverbs 20:20 says, "If a man curses his father or mother, his lamp will be snuffed out in pitch darkness." Think of it! One of the reasons I may be unable to experience a greater indwelling of the presence of Christ, one of the reasons I may be unable to hear from God when I most desperately need to, is that I have cursed my father and my mother!

Can we prodigal brothers, who stand upon the pedestal of righteousness and perfection, be made to see the depth of our sin? We're mad at the sibling who did what he knew was wrong and didn't care, didn't care that Mom and Dad were devastated by his choices, didn't care the whole family was turned into a chaotic mess by his behavior. That frustration is compounded by the fact that our parents may not have seemed to care about doing what would work. We who are so perfect, who see maybe not exactly *what* should be done but *what should result* when right things are done, are filled with hatred and lie to ourselves about what it is! How will we ever understand that the ceaseless love of the Father, characterized by he who paced and prayed and wept and waited and watched and expected the prodigal to return, is poured out toward us because we are just as sick and diseased inside as our debauched and polluted brother? Like the painting in Oscar Wilde's *The Picture of Dorian Gray*, we maintain an outward cleanliness while in the back room of our souls sits the stinking, rotting effects of our own sin. If we say we love God, we must love our brother, our sister, our mother, our father.

Helmut Thielicke wrote that Jesus was able to love the worst of humanity "only because he saw through the filth and crust of degeneration, because his eye caught the divine original which is hidden in every way—in *every* man! . . . First and foremost he gives us new eyes. . . .

"When Jesus loved a guilt-laden person and helped him, he saw in him an erring child of God. He saw in him a human being whom his Father loved and grieved over because he was going wrong. He saw him as God originally designed and meant him to be, and therefore he saw through the surface layer of grime and dirt to the real man underneath. . . . Jesus was able to love men because he loved them right through the layer of mud."[6]

I cannot do it on my own. I cannot see my brother through the layer of mud without the eyes of Jesus. I cannot see my parents through the residue of their errors without the eyes that Jesus will give me when I run to the cross to lay down my own dark, clotted mud. In Matthew 7:1-2, we read these words of Jesus: "Do not judge, or you too will be judged. For in the same way you judge others, you will be judged, and with the measure you use, it will be measured to you." How would you prefer to be judged? With all the facts at hand, with your feelings considered, with compassion? Then judge that way, Jesus was saying. His context referred to judging done hypocritically or self-righteously. If we judge others with a standard that does not recognize our own sinfulness, we will judge in a manner that implies—that shouts!—we are not sinful. He continued, "Why do you look at the speck of sawdust in your brother's eye and pay no attention to the plank in your own eye? . . . You *hypocrite*," Jesus said (emphasis mine), "first take the plank out of your own eye, and then you will see clearly to remove the speck from your brother's eye." I like this paraphrase from *The Message*: "Do you have the nerve to say, 'Let me wash our face for you,' when your own face is distorted by contempt?"

Jesus dealt with a culture that held there were those who were morally flawless—the doctors of the Law—and were thus entitled to point out to any and all the failings that made people unacceptable to God. But the only way to effectively assist someone else in seeing his or her sin, He explained to the people, was to have a full understanding of one's own mud! He did not say, "Don't ever tell someone else they have a speck in their eye, because then you're acting morally superior." What He did say was, "You have a big log in your eye. *Remove it first.*"

What effect would removing my log have on addressing my brother's speck? If I knew the pain of removing a massive object from my eye—if I were well aware of the surgery-without-anesthesia panic of pulling a foreign body out of my eyeball—how would I approach someone with only a speck? You can be sure I would not attempt to use locking pliers when a slim pair of tweezers would do. And hands working on delicate eyes need to be gentle and patient lest the eye be damaged. Remember—it's not the eye that's the problem, it's the speck! Pulling out specks is difficult, painstaking work requiring wisdom and skill.

When I have a speck in my eye, by what measure would I prefer to be judged? The measure that acknowledges that even though I have done wrong, I am loved. God is eager to forgive, waiting for me, ready to help me move on. I do not want to be judged by the measure of someone else's unrighteous criticism, flowing from resentment or anger or arrogance. Sometimes I marvel at how hard we work to justify ourselves. Wouldn't it be simply wonderful if we could be completely free and honest about our failings, thanking God for His provision? I have to admit that I'm no better than my parents. I have my arrogance to deal with, my hurtful criticisms, my withering contempt. Knowing all this, my goal is to be able to agree without defensiveness with the person who points these things out to me.

"The eye is the lamp of the body. If your eyes are good, your whole body will be full of light. But if your eyes are bad, your whole body will be full of darkness. If then the light within you is darkness, how great is that darkness!" (Matthew 6:22-23). I must search for that way from the darkness outside the house into the light, so that I can be full of light. There is so much more going on in this drama than just my hurt feelings! God wants to make me as brightly lit as a house with a party going on inside of it. He doesn't just invite me inside to celebrate; He wants me to be the living representation of that joyful gathering. He wants my every step to ring with the music of feasting and delight! He wants this house to draw others to Himself, just as Jesus did.

Something is required of me to turn this house into a magnet for hurting people looking for warmth and compassion and sustenance, for forgiveness and acceptance. It is the necessity of setting aside my resentments and letting God do the big thing He so desires to do. Curtis and Eldredge explain, "Every human being is of great significance to God, but those whom God has drawn to believe in him are center stage in a drama of cosmic proportions."[7] This life's little struggle, this "light affliction," as Paul put it, is just a thread in the bigger tapestry our Father is weaving. So much is going on around us, unseen, working to keep us focused on the emotions sewn into our pasts. We can't see it until we step out of the darkness into the light, where our sight will be clear and the awful darkness that would keep us cold and alone will be dispelled.

— CHAPTER NINE —

Trust and Gratitude

The question before us is simply: What can we do to make the return possible? Although God himself runs out to us to find us and bring us home, we must not only recognize that we are lost, but also be prepared to be found and brought home. How? Obviously not by just waiting and being passive. Although we are incapable of liberating ourselves from our frozen anger, we can allow ourselves to be found by God and healed by his love through the concrete and daily practice of trust and gratitude. Trust and gratitude are the disciplines for the conversion of the elder son.

—HENRI NOUWEN[1]

My parents may not have been able to do everything well, but they knew how to say, "I love you." They may not have understood sometimes words are not enough to reach the deepest levels of the heart, but they were generous with frequent expressions and displays of affection. Some people may have experienced parents who subscribed to a kind of clairvoyant love, expressed in comments such as, "I go out and work for a living every day—you ought to know that means I love you." Clairvoyant love expects others to read the mind of the thinker, to "just know" love is intended. It's true some people show their love by actions, but someone forever unable to *say* the words must to recognize those close to him may need to *hear* something with their ears!

I heard so many times my father's story of when he first saw me I can retell it verbatim. I smile at the memory of my mother telling me countless times of how she thrilled to becoming an "instant mother." Accounts of how much I was adored are firmly planted in my mind and I believe them without reservation because they were spoken of passionately, with conviction, often related with tears, and always concluded with a hug.

We read in the parable the father had a heart that could be "filled with compassion." He was a man who could embrace his returning child by throwing his arms around him after picking up the skirt of his robes and running to meet him. Running was not a typical practice of dignified Middle Eastern men, and as Jesus told the story to the crowd around Him, this detail emphasized the father's powerful explosion of joy. Lack of love is not the problem. There may be prodigal brothers out there who lived with indifferent or unaffectionate parents; every story is personal, and each of us has had specific challenges. But it is usually desperate, self-sacrificing love that drives parents to believe if they just give enough, if they are simply willing to suffer enough to prove their love to the prodigal, everything will work out in the end. It may not work, but that does not mean love was not present.

The truth is one can be deeply loved and systematically ignored. It's not intentional. Parents don't sit down and plan to give all of their energies to one child, expecting the others to understand and hang in there until the tough times are over. But children need to know someone knows them, *wants* to know them. I never doubted I was loved, but I was never sure I *mattered*. A friend of mine who abused drugs during her teenage years told me she is positive her sister, who essentially took care of the family during that awful period, had to wonder to herself, "Do I have to take drugs to get noticed around here?"

For a long time after I became a Christian, when going to the Lord in prayer I pictured myself walking into God's presence, hearing the heels of my shoes *click-click* upon a marble floor. I'd approach the great throne and stand in front of an altar, knowing with certainty I was a child of God and I had an advocate with the Father, Jesus Christ the Righteous. I knew I could ask of my Father anything in Jesus' name, and He would answer me compassionately and empathetically, because my Bible told me so and all the preaching and teaching I'd heard confirmed it. But even though I knew this and believed it, in my mind's eye I always saw the Lord God Almighty lift His head and look my way with anticipation, and when realizing it was me, heard Him say glumly, "Oh—*you* again?"

This expectation was so ingrained within me that it was many years into my walk with the Lord before I realized where it came from. I thought I was just essentially insecure, which was partly true. But that perception of being a disappointment to God, that He was anticipating someone more important, more exciting, more interesting than I, was a product of the knowledge that for my folks, what was going on with me was just not as big as what was going on with my brother. No matter how spectacular my accomplishments, I couldn't get a wholehearted acclamation.

Knowing I was loved, knowing my brother was impaired, knowing my parents were limited and did the best they could— none of this could heal the hole in my heart needing the embrace of recognition. No matter how much I understood the facts and wanted to forgive, the loneliness of being the "good" child who gave the parents permission to exert all of their energies on the difficult one had become part of the internal needlework of my life. I just kept working harder, performing better, waiting for a moment of clear, untainted acknowledgment from my parents. It came rarely and was not enough, and I traveled to a distant land, placing my hurt between myself and my family. My efforts and my judgments were my possessions, my comforters, my prizes. I built monuments to my own rightness and tried to get along without my family.

In addition to feeling ignored and invisible, some of us also grew up with discouraging words and actions. Many years ago, I was speaking at a series of church meetings in New York and the woman with whom I was staying rented the movie *Rudy* for us to watch on the one night there was no service. What a lesson is contained in that film! The story of a young man from an economically struggling Catholic family who dreamed of going to the University of Notre Dame and playing for its famed football team, it chronicles his determination to push back against every formidable obstacle. Small in stature, he seems unable to see himself in the mirror and face facts: he is physically all wrong for college football. In addition, he can't seem to accept his limited intellect cannot be honed enough to get him into such a prestigious school. He's positively blind with the belief he can get what he wants if he's willing to work hard enough. *(Spoiler alert! If you haven't seen the movie, I'm about to give away the ending in the next few paragraphs.)*

After tremendous struggle, including deflecting the nasty negativism of his older brother and his father's sad urging to just accept life's limitations, Rudy makes it to Notre Dame! He immediately volunteers for the football team, coached by the legendary Ara Parsigian, and is practically laughed off the field.

One of the coaches sees his grit and gives him a place on the practice team while another coach argues Rudy will never make it through the grueling exercises. In one agonizing practice after another, we see Rudy hammered, pummeled, thrashed, squashed, and battered. Each time, he walks more slowly to the showers, bloodied and sick with pain. The players snicker behind his back, sure he will never return. They are amazed, and some are angered, when he gives his all on the practice field as though he had arrived in town only yesterday.

A grudging respect begins to build for the little bulldog who will not give up. He steps out on a limb and requests of Coach Parsigian permission to dress for a game and simply sit on the bench to show his family he really *is* a member of the Fighting Irish. Rudy's father is thrilled he made it into Notre Dame but he sees no value in his son's desire to further prove himself. His brother has discouraged him every step of the way in spite of Rudy's accomplishments, and tells him none of it means anything unless he actually gets in the game. Not one word of praise, not one indication of pride or joy at his little brother's fierce determination. Rudy desperately wants to show them both his dreams have come true, that he has *made* them come true.

The final game of Rudy's senior year approaches, and circumstances have occurred suggesting Rudy may not make it to the field with the varsity team. He scrutinizes the list of those who are to play and cannot find his name. It appears at last he must admit defeat. He walks away, dejected, and his fellow players, who have now come to love this little man who puts them all to shame with his dedication, take note. In one of those gloriously tear-jerking movie scenes, each player selected for the final game, starting with the captain of the team, enters the head coach's office and lays his numbered jersey on the coach's desk, asking that Rudy be allowed to suit up in his place.

The end of the movie is positively triumphant, all the more so because it is a true story. Rudy's parents and brother make the long trip for the game. His brother is disbelieving until the moment he sees Rudy lead the team onto the field, and is simply incredulous when Rudy is called into the game during its crucial last moments. All of the agony and suffering and torture of practice, the building of determination and commitment, pays off for Rudy, and he runs with his team to secure victory, becoming the truest symbol of Fighting Irish tenacity.

A man's father or mother or brother can strike him down or lift him up. A woman's father or mother or sister can make her feel inadequate or encourage her best abilities. Parents want to propel us to do great things, and they sometimes cannot accept we are not inspired by the negative. They use reverse psychology in trying to motivate us, and can't understand the discouraging words sit in us like stones at the bottom of a pond.

I think of little Rudy Rudiger of Notre Dame, who never should have made it to college at all, much less the college of his dreams. I think of the fire that burned within him to make it onto the football team, and how he took every blow, every bone-crushing collision, who felt with even greater force the utter sadness of his working-class father whose dreams had died and who seemed intent on making sure his son's would die, too. Rudy wanted to bring his father some pride, some joy, return to him the hope he must have once had. Rudy got knocked down, but he got up. Consider the words of Paul: "We are hard pressed on every side, but not crushed; perplexed, but not in despair; persecuted, but not abandoned; struck down, but not destroyed. . . . For our light and momentary troubles are achieving for us an eternal glory that far outweighs them all. So we fix our eyes not on what is seen, but on what is unseen. For what is seen is temporary, but what is unseen is eternal" (2 Corinthians 4:8-9, 17-18).

We have to push the boulders off of our lives and *get up*. There's no point anymore in blaming those who threw the stones. We're the ones who make the decision to sleep or to rise. Both have consequences in the present and for eternity.

The wise father of the parable receives his son's accusation and then speaks simply to the core of his hurt and tells him he is a beloved son: "You have always been with me, and everything

I have is yours." This remark speaks volumes. In those words is the father's affirmation the son is wanted in the house and the father has never felt otherwise. In those words is devotion and acceptance and recognition, elements the heart of the son longs to hear—needs to hear—and, if he really hears them, will reach to the original bruise.

Then the father explains to the son in a profound declaration that this event is not about him. It's not about the family. It's not about who was right and who was wrong. "We have to celebrate and be glad," he says simply, "because your brother was dead and now he is alive again." In this one statement, the father impresses upon his son the party celebrates not the immediate, but the eternal. Yes, there are immediate concerns, and we will deal with them—trust me, the father might have communicated. Trust me that I know you. Trust me that I see what's been happening to your heart. Right now, though, let's be grateful your brother has been found. There's a larger purpose here, a bigger picture.

We must understand God has a higher agenda. He sees the entire view of human workings and failings and polluted reactions and emotions, and through this parable, He explains *we must be willing to see that view along with Him*. It's not just about us and our hurt feelings. It's not just about our righteous indignation. It's about the heart of a father who runs to his wayward son and expects the older son, who remains with him and shares in all the benefits of the relationship, to understand the bigger purpose and rejoice with him. The father wants the older son to see as he sees, to look past the immediate and come up higher, where the whole valley of pain and suffering can be seen from the mountain of forgiveness and compassion. He invites us to trust Him that everything will have a purpose in the end. If I can grab on to that trust somehow, if I can hold it to my heart and know my Father wants me at the celebration, I can take a step.

Trust and gratitude are the two feet that will carry me toward the house where the party is in process. Trust and gratitude are the two eyes that will see my Father as He strides toward me, arms outstretched, urging me to join Him in celebration. They are the two hands that will grasp my Father's cloak so I can walk with Him to the house where forgiveness permeates the atmosphere and I can find rest from my demand to be heard and congratulated for my righteousness. Only trust that my Father sees me fully and knows me completely, and gratitude for the orchestration of the events of my life He knows will best serve His plans, can provide for me the spark of desire that will cause me to *want* to lay aside all that has happened, all who have hurt me, all I let wound me.

Does my heavenly Father know what I have carried in the deepest crevices of my heart? Yes. Can I trust He has watched the scenes of despair in my family and understands what they created in me? He knows it all, but asks me to consider it of lesser priority than the opportunity to follow Him to a higher place where He can show me what He desires to accomplish. Once I am there with Him, viewing the picture He sees, I can be grateful for my history and use it to maintain the freedom of forgiveness. Gratefulness will keep me from falling back into the darkness outside the house.

Gratitude will give me the momentum to continue. I will focus my attention on the love I was given and be grateful for the good. I rehearse the stories in my memories that remind me my parents cared for me, that they were once a romantic young couple desiring a child. I keep my eyes on the memories that cause me to smile. I recall the lessons they taught me, the laughter we shared, my mother's marvelous stories, the tenderness of my father as he cared for me when I was sick. I watch home movies and remind myself of the precious little brother who would perform the dizzying spins I demonstrated, who tried to keep up with me as we jumped on swings in the park. These things shaped me, too, just as much as the hard and injurious transgressions. That I am able to see the effects of the events of my life upon the shaping of my personality is God's gift to me, and I must spend time in grateful reflection to maintain the integrity of forgiveness. "Finally, brothers, whatever is true, whatever is noble, whatever is right, whatever is pure, whatever is lovely, whatever is admirable—if anything is excellent or praiseworthy—think about such things" (Philippians 4:8).

Some prodigal brothers may have few recollections of good things on which to meditate. I urge them to fix upon even one, and to contemplate that one good thing until they have turned it over and examined it from all sides, until they know its length and width and height and depth, until it is worn to softness and fits perfectly in the palm of their hand. The Holy Spirit will use all of our grateful offerings to illuminate the underlying reasons for the things we experienced and expand our capacity to cover over a multitude of sins with love. He will show us how we were braided into the texture of our families. He will show us why we were there.

Every time I read the parable I am moved because I see the father perceiving the different needs of his two very different sons. One son needed to be received after making a long journey home, and the father was waiting with the door open and an expression of true forgiveness. The other son needed to be received after walking in from working for recognition to find his relationship to the father was significant enough to justify an appeal to his sensitivities. The father didn't hesitate to offer himself in the way each son required.

My heavenly Father sees me, and He has come out and urged me to walk with Him into the house where the celebration for prodigals is in full swing. The prodigal son is already there, and his prodigal brother is on the way.

— CHAPTER TEN —

The Light Will Reveal

If the Spirit of God detects anything in you that is wrong, He does not ask you to put it right; He asks you to accept the light, and He will put it right. A child of the light confesses instantly and stands bared before God; a child of the darkness says—"Oh, I can explain that away." When once the light breaks and the conviction of wrong comes, be a child of the light, and confess, and God will deal with what is wrong; if you vindicate yourself, you prove yourself to be a child of the darkness.

—OSWALD CHAMBERS[1]

Have you ever stepped into a room in the soft light of evening and been impressed with how neat and tidy the room appears to be? You wake up the next morning and go about your routine, finally opening the curtains to the bright light of day, and you're startled by the amount of dust you see. What was impossible to see in evening's light is now strikingly obvious. No matter how lovely the room looked in soft light, the introduction of bright light showed it was unclean.

Light has found its way into the room of my personal story and is revealing dust that has collected year after year, the results of my family's tragic tale: Anger. Depression. Abandonment. Loneliness. My bitterness toward my family is a cancer, and the arrogance of considering myself so much better than they is a tumor of pride and conceit. "Do not think of yourselves more highly than you ought," wrote Paul to the Corinthians, and sometimes I can't figure out *what* I should think of myself. I have viewed myself as sitting upon a mountain of better thinking, placing myself above them with my foot on their necks. I hate that my brother made life so difficult and that my parents couldn't address it thoughtfully. I hate that I've felt like an alien in the place where I was supposed to feel I belonged. I could make myself sick with the telling of injustices, until, like the Israelites who ate their fill of quail in the desert, the taste of my demands filled me to disgust. I cannot deny my hate because the light has come to reveal it.

The Apostle John said, "God is light; in him is no darkness at all. If we claim to have fellowship with him yet walk in the darkness, we lie and do not live by the truth. But if we walk in the light, as he is in the light, we have fellowship with one another, and the blood of Jesus, his Son, purifies us from all sin. If we claim to be without sin, we deceive ourselves and the truth is not in us. If we confess our sins, he is faithful and just and will forgive us our sins and purify us from all unrighteousness. If we claim we have not sinned, we make him out to be a liar and his word has no place in our lives" (1 John 1:5-10).

What does it mean to walk in the light? How do I know I'm doing it? The Bible tells me I am a member of the kingdom of light. "You are all sons of the light and sons of the day. We do not belong to the night or to the darkness" (1 Thessalonians 5:5). I used to hold on to my darkness, permitting it to create a fabric for my thoughts. I allowed it to remain because it was comfortable and familiar. I could sink into it and stroke my wounds. But now light defines me. If I claim to belong to Him who reveals Himself in light and continue to take refuge in my dark comfort, John says I'm a liar. To prefer darkness is diametrically opposed to the day rising within me. I can't stand with one foot in the day and one foot in the night. God's light is all-or-nothing.

Light is hot, sometimes uncomfortably so. It highlights imperfections, dispels the shadows to which our eyes have adjusted, and can be painful in its intensity. Light—directed, concentrated light—is used in surgery. In skilled hands, a laser can burn away a cancerous growth or slice a cornea in precisely the right places, freeing the body from disease or setting vision aright. Light guides missiles to target. It melts ice. It transmits data, burns skin, detects a fractured bone or a hidden gun, and influences our internal body clock.

Light provides direction and is our hope at the end of a tunnel of difficult times. It displays things we long to see. It unveils squalid surroundings we would prefer to ignore. I'm reminded of Ric Burns's marvelous documentary *New York*, in which a segment is dedicated to the work of late-19th-century newspaper reporter Jacob Riis. Riis had once fallen on hard times and was lost among the poverty-stricken, and after he had regained his footing he was haunted by the wretched circumstances he had witnessed. He *needed* to tell what he had seen, what had become his personal fire-shut-up-in-my-bones message. In 1890, Riis went through the tenements of the Lower East Side with a cameraman and took picture after picture of the sickening conditions of immigrant life. The flash powder that had just been invented allowed him to illuminate the horrifying world of the city's poor. His book,

How the Other Half Lives, stunned all who picked it up and leafed through its pages. The revulsion and shame New Yorkers felt when viewing the photographs and reading his descriptions sparked a movement of social change that benefited those who had been invisible, dying, disregarded, until an illuminating flare exposed their plight. Light reveals, proclaims, mobilizes.

When I ask Christ to be the Ruler of my life, light enters in and makes visible every hidden thing. When the Father travels through my insides and directs His ferocious beacon upon areas I have ignored or forgotten, it is because He is pulling me into His kind of life. I'm being cleaned out. All of the old life is being cataloged for delivery to the foot of the cross. Before I experienced salvation, few of my actions seemed to me to be sinful. I thought, "I'm a good person. I haven't murdered anyone, I don't steal." I read "sinful" as "criminal" and since I wasn't a criminal, I deemed myself good. Living in a world of shadows made it possible for me to ignore the deeper implications of my thoughts and behavior. Now they must be tagged and removed.

I have a photograph of my brother and myself standing on a neighbor's lawn some time after we moved to Los Angeles. Taller than he, I have my arm around him and we are smiling the charming grins of kids who love to have their picture taken. From that picture-taking point on, our family went slowly haywire, although I know things were smoldering before then. Before we left West Virginia my brother was enthralled by the older boy next door, a cruel and vicious son of a father just the same. My brother picked up a lot from this kid, and I wonder how much my mom and dad saw it. This was an early influence upon my brother, who was a boy easily led into the drug-like thrill of wrongdoing.

The photograph of the two of us speaks to me of the last unencumbered time before I felt my family begin to disintegrate. It was summer and I remember us as happy then, still excited about our new lives in Southern California. But soon I sensed the landscape changing, the energies shifting, my parents turning their attention to the needy child. In the years to come, I trained my heart to shut down when troubles arose. I escaped to the library, where I spent long hours evading the sad atmosphere of my home. It was my refuge around the corner, where I read of smart people who did smart things and I decided somehow I would get away from what awaited me one block over.

Other folks can tell of pledges made in far more beastly hours, when evils committed set a part of their hearts in concrete and destroyed irreplaceable innocence and trust. I don't know when my vows sprang up, when their vines wrapped about my internal network and began to bear the fruit of my judgments. I just know I became disgusted, furious, superior, and determined to take care of myself. Such things had been fermenting inside for a long time, and no matter what evil created them, they took on an evil of their own. They are sin. Now light has come to pull them out of hiding and burn them away.

How I would love to present myself to my Father and tell Him of my life and have Him say to me, "You poor thing! What a horrible situation! I don't know how you put up with it!" I'd love for Him to tell me I have every right to hate my brother into eternity and grind my teeth at my parents' inadequacies. How satisfying it would be to hear Him agree with my condemnations and join me in clucking over the mess I had to endure.

But I know He is El-Shaddai, Almighty God, and He will not empathize with sin. I know what is good and perfect and righteous gives no place to self-congratulatory consolation, and I can't get away with expecting the Lord to sympathize with my darkness. He *does* have tenderness for my pain. He knows what I lived through, He knows the damage I sustained and He pours His love upon me like a healing oil to soften the scabs of my resentment. But He pulls me into the light as He is in the light and urges me to unburden myself of all the hindrances that will prevent me from full and open communication with Him. The writer of Hebrews encourages us to "throw off everything that hinders and the sin that so easily entangles, and let us run with perseverance the race marked out for us. Let us fix our eyes on Jesus, the author and perfecter of our faith, who for the joy set before him endured the cross, scorning its shame, and sat down at the right hand of the throne of God" (12:1-2). I have to do the work of throwing off what has entangled me. He provides the light to see the hindrances. It's not a fearful thing to have them exposed; it's a loving invitation to freedom.

"You were taught, with regard to your former way of life, to put off your old self, which is being corrupted by its deceitful desires; to be made new in the attitude of your minds; and to put on the new self, created to be like God in true righteousness and holiness" (Ephesians 4:22-24). That former way of life has got to go, and so each element must be drawn into the light, placed in a lineup and selected for prosecution. I'm not to defend them, not to explain my reasons for attachment, because no matter what the background, they are wrong and now must be discarded for what is right. I want them out on the altar, right in front of Jesus Who took the penalty for all of the grime within me and Who loves me beyond measure.

Like any believer, I want to do what is right. I want to take delight in my walk with the Lord and find pleasure in new life. But I know vindictive rage still resides here. I can still taste my desire for retribution. I still want an apology. I think of Elijah, who ran and hid and then cried to the Lord that he was all alone and unappreciated. He was commanded, " 'Go out and stand on the mountain in the presence of the LORD, for the LORD is about to pass by.' Then a great and powerful wind tore the mountains apart and shattered the rocks before the LORD, but the LORD was not in the wind. After the wind there was an earthquake, but the LORD was not in the earthquake. After the earthquake came a fire, but the LORD was not in the fire. And after the fire came a gentle whisper" (1 Kings 19:11-12).

Growing up in Los Angeles, I experienced powerful winds, mudslides, fires, and earthquakes. A quake seems filled with a terrifying kind of life; it roars. I've been through a couple of big ones and can tell you that after a few horrific moments of shaking, it's hard to move. Elijah heard rocks shattering and felt the ground rolling, and I wonder if his body's flight responses failed him, because he remained in the cave. When all was quiet, he sat in the silence and waited.

For those of us who have been touched by some form of tragedy, the noise and the motion of our pasts roars at us to remain in the cave and protect ourselves from further injury. But God is not in those voices. He's not in the bitterness and He won't participate in the flagellation we wrongly expect will bring us relief. He's not in the rock-throwing and the blowhard excuses we spew out in defense of our stunted growth. He's not in the flame of offense and He won't provide the oxygen to keep it burning. We do that. All of those things are our doing, and He's not in them. He's in the gentle whisper. "When Elijah heard it, he pulled his cloak over his face and went out and stood at the mouth of the cave. Then a voice said to him, 'What are you doing here, Elijah?' " (v. 13).

God wants to know what *we* think we're doing and where *we* think we're going. When we say it out loud, we reveal the motives of our hearts. Many months after my mother died, as I pondered our difficult relationship, I blurted out to my husband (without thinking about what I was about to say), "Now that my mother is gone, I have no opportunity to prove to her how wrong she was!" Here was my life's motivation, hidden in personal indignation over all I had suffered: to finally, somehow, emphatically prove to my mother she was *wrong about everything*.

Elijah heard the gentle whisper and it drew him out of his hiding place. We are not set free by sitting in the darkness in the back of a cave where we're nursing the original bruise. This is not the behavior of free people! Playing the pain over and over will never make us whole. It will keep us captive. It will take us in its teeth and thrash us in a wild frenzy. The more we determine to behave differently, the more it asserts itself in unexpected moments, proving to us *it owns us* and we will never be rid of it. Only light can burn it out, and we must walk into the light. The intensity and discomfort of the light will never equal the weight of the hurt within us. When we take a deep breath and say, "Boots, start walking," we discover the light is a beautiful thing.

The gentle voice doesn't condemn or punish. It doesn't need to, because when we see what we are doing, the shame pretty much lays us out like a boxer who's just taken one in the gut. Once we're used to these revelations, we run to the light for purifying. Like a sore muscle being massaged, it hurts so *good*. Healing is always the result! The gentle voice calls to us to rise and approach the doorway into light.

Elijah stood in the light and revealed his innermost thoughts. He was not struck dead. His ministry was not taken from him, nor was his heavenly anointing lifted. He was given direction just as Hagar was. God is not desiring to punish us. He's working to perfect us! He doesn't need to stick pins in us and tell us over and over how worthless we are to Him. We do that to ourselves, and when we assign our voice to Him, thinking the Lord is castigating us, we're giving our enemy a weapon. Only Satan accuses. The Father just keeps pulling us into the light.

I haven't been left to decay! The light has made its way to me and I see my sin. I see my need for forgiveness; I see the prescription to forgive. The fact that I *want* to forgive, that I know I need to forgive, that I am aware of the emotional affliction I still feel from events long past, is the evidence *He is pulling me into the light*. He does not want me to rest in the residue of my former life. If I want to stay there, I will have to actively resist Him. I will find myself fighting to retreat into darkness, and it is a fight for death.

I know the light is drawing me simply because I do not deny what I know is true. I *know* what my sin is doing to me. I *know* if I do not expose it, it will eat away at me and erode my honest and uninterrupted communication with my Savior. I live by the truth now. I am a child of the day. "For you were once darkness, but now you are light in the Lord. Live as children of light (for the fruit of the light consists in all goodness, righteousness and truth) and find out what pleases the Lord" (Ephesians 5:8-10).

As a child of the light, I can instantly identify the sins approaching in the road. When jealousy steps out from behind an event, I know what it is because I can see it clearly. When meanness, or spite, or hostility—any number of corrupt attitudes—tries to overtake me on the way, I can see them coming. I clearly see rage and do not mistake it for disappointment. Hatred can't disguise itself as indifference; manipulation can't masquerade as loving concern. The light has made my eyes merciless. I can't even pretend certain feelings or behaviors don't bother me; light has exposed them and made them plain. When I speak arrogantly, I hear the pride, and when I would prefer to color my disgust in softer tones I have no excuse but to see it as anything but stark and unforgiving contempt. When we walk in the light, we will not struggle with the hidden sins of darkness. They will have no place to hide.

I may be dismayed at what I see rising to the surface—the deep impurities of sin—but they are rising because they are scheduled for destruction. I see them, and I confess them, and I am forgiven because He is faithful to His own word. Walking in the light makes my relationship with the Lord clear and without deception. In one of those lovely consequences of His grace, it does the same for my relationships with others.

When we drive at night along dark roads, landmarks and signs are difficult to see. Our headlights can only illuminate so much, and we miss the turnoff that would be obvious in the day, or the narrow street we'd find easily when the sun is up. Relationships can be similarly hard to negotiate. We miss hints and misunderstand intentions. We claim innocence when we are guilty, demand perfection when we are flawed, and dismiss emotions when we are seething with reproach. We drive miles past those we love, unable to see the simplest indicators because the darkness of sinful complaints has obscured our vision. Like wearing glasses smeared with grime, we see nothing clearly—not our loved ones, not ourselves, not God. It's through these lenses we are trying to see well enough to navigate our lives.

For decades, I massaged the aches of my heart created in the sad dysfunction of my family. Some of the aches were burned away when I met Christ and others have been burned away as I've walked with Him, but many times I knelt in prayer, hating myself for my contempt of my family, guilt oozing from every spiritual pore. I always knew my judgments were hard and I was carrying a boulder of "ungrace," as Philip Yancey puts it, within my heart. When light permeates, those waves of energy bounce back and indicate there's something lodged deep within. No matter how clean I may have felt after some marvelous spiritual experience, my fury at my parents and my brother still had a heartbeat. I couldn't kill it. But those deep, persistent offenses must have the spotlight of God's love focused upon them so I can haul them to the cross. It's time to stop railing at my family, like Balaam thrashing his little donkey, who cried out to him, "What have I done to you to make you beat me?" They were traveling with the knowledge and dispositions they had. I must lay down the stick of my own righteousness and stop flailing at the helpless and the weak.

If the Light is living in me, He will pull me into Himself, into His kingdom, into His very substance; and little by little, what once gave me pleasure ceases to call to me. What I formerly considered acceptable now leaves a horrid taste in my mouth. The real me is raised from the dead, and I discover myself becoming more confident in what God has placed in me, less afraid to trust Him. He walks through the rooms of my spirit, opening doors and windows, pushing back the internal shadows that should have no place within me. It's there in those rooms I have hidden my resentments and my pain. It's there I've closed the door on my judgments and my hatreds. The Holy Spirit drags them out into the light where they can be seen in all of their wickedness. I discover He desires to rework my life, making me different inside.

The Lord does not stop at forgiving me only—He wants to see me changed, a reflection of the brightness of His glory.

I can hear a celebration going on in the distance. I see a house lit up with merriment. It's drawing me. That's where I want to go.

— CHAPTER ELEVEN —

My Machine of Hideous Beauty

O my son Absalom! My son, my son Absalom! If only I had died instead of you—O Absalom, my son, my son!

—2 SAMUEL 18:33

While out of town on a short vacation, I called home to see if there were any messages on our answering machine. There were three or four—all of them from my father, who had forgotten we were away, calling for Larry to pick up the phone, asking him to call. Finally he said, "Sue's brother has died. He died in his sleep." I heard his long silence, and then, "Please call." Danny had succumbed to undiagnosed and untreated cardiomyopathy, his heart further weakened by decades of drug and alcohol abuse.

Only a few years before, my mother had died from the result of an injury sustained during a surgical procedure. As in so many marriages of their generation, my mother was the one who kept all of the connections. She stayed in communication with family, mailed Christmas cards to friends, wrote letters to distant acquaintances, called me every weekend. After my mother died, I felt I lost my father, too. He never called unless I called him. He spoke frequently of his love for different relatives, but never tried to reach them. He'd ask how different family members were faring, and I'd tell him how much they would enjoy a call from him. He would always agree and then do nothing. Most did not call him, either, and so he slowly lost all contact with the people he had held dear and was as cut off from his lifelong relations as though he had died himself. When Mom died, his conduit to everything outside of himself was severed.

Dad married very soon after losing my mother. Shortly afterward, my brother came stumbling back into the picture, and Dad committed himself to him as though giving his life to my brother was his last necessary work. His new wife, who had expected a companion, was justifiably appalled when he moved in with Danny to take care of him. He poured money and time and effort into him and ended up being cussed out and vilified in the middle of the night as Danny succumbed to illness. Alternating between railing at my father and sobbing in discomfort and fear of death, my brother had been experiencing back pain that made it almost impossible for him to walk. Neither my dad nor my brother seriously pursued diagnosis and treatment. As far as I know, the only doctor they saw was one in a local emergency room. X-rays of my brother's back showed nothing unusual, and that was as far as any investigation went. I think they were both too frightened of what the cause might be and simply did not want to find out. My brother had always been so terrified of death he considered any pain a symptom of impending doom, and now he was suffering severely.

My father would listen to my suggestions regarding doctors and tests and then tell me how my brother would wake up in the middle of the night, shouting his demand that my father help him to the bathroom, hurling vile abuse at him as he was nearly carried back to bed. As he would get my brother settled again, the mood would change and there would be a brief period of quiet discussion in which my brother would ask my father about heaven, about whether God might allow him to enter, about whether he would see Mom again. My dad would talk to him about the Lord Jesus and sometimes they'd pray together.

One night after several months of this awful routine, my father awoke around 2:00 a.m. expecting to hear the usual harsh command. He waited, and waited . . . and all was silent. He knew something had changed. "It took me nearly an hour to get up the courage to go and check on him," he told me, my heart breaking for him. "I went in and called his name. I finally walked to the bed and touched him, and I knew he was gone."

We had taken my mother's ashes and buried them on her mother's grave in West Virginia, and now Dad brought my brother's and we did the same. A few family members met us at the cemetery, and we made our way up the long hill after reading some Bible verses and saying a prayer. As my cousin's husband dug a small depression, I began singing "Just As I Am," and soon we were done. After that, the man had nothing left to give him the desire to hold on to life.

It was my brother's death that cut the last rope that kept him from drifting into isolation. My father's memory began to deteriorate alarmingly. His short-term memory had been fading, but his neurologist was unwilling to diagnose Alzheimer's because he experienced pain from another condition, and pain coupled with depression can have a strong impact upon memory. My dad knew who people were and could identify his surroundings, but he could not remember a discussion he'd had days or even hours earlier. He could mostly take care of himself, and so it seemed some sort of dementia was at work, but we hoped it was not Alzheimer's disease. It was.

When I think of the blows my father experienced in such a short period I feel how heavy and destructive they were for him. When my mother was taken he lost any psychological ballast that would prevent him from sinking. Then, with my brother's death, a hole was blown in the hull of his fragile personality. Terrified of experiencing strong emotions, incapable of expressing them freely, he ran as hard and as fast as he could from them and so never grieved my mother or my brother sufficiently to be able to face the world again. With all that life-pounding trauma, he was lost to me. I would send cards telling him I'd love to hear from him and would wait in vain for a call. I once let nearly six months pass before I contacted him by phone, wondering if he'd ever get in touch with me on his own. I finally called on his birthday. Time seemed to have collapsed for him; as far as he was concerned we had chatted just a couple of weeks before.

My heart hurt for his loneliness and pain and his deep insecurity. My husband tells me he's never known anyone with so many personal demons as my father. His fear of a full life was tangible. I sensed the confusion that slowly engulfed him, month following month, as he forgot so many things, dropped so many important details, and began losing control, control it seems he'd never really exhibited to begin with.

My parents were not some kind of aberration. There are all kinds of instructions and admonitions in the Bible about how to raise children, but even the great characters of old, those we would expect would have done everything right, made fatal mistakes.

King David, Israel's most beloved king, was called a man after God's own heart (Acts 13:22), and was the royal progenitor of the Messiah. Even so, David was an ineffective and irresponsible father to his sons and suffered the judgment of it. In 2 Samuel, we read of one of David's sons, Amnon, who raped his half-sister, Tamar. When David did nothing, her brother, Absalom, who took Tamar into his home where she lived as "a desolate woman," seethed at this injustice and eventually murdered Amnon in revenge. David forgave Absalom without requiring any sort of repentance, but his forgiveness did not change his son's ways. Absalom then rebelled in the most open and humiliating of ways, having long carried churning resentment against his father.

David's love for his son paralyzed him. Amnon *raped* Tamar. Absalom *murdered* his brother. David, the warrior king, the emotional worshiper, the man who had led legions into battle and danced with abandon when the ark was returned to Israel, seemed utterly powerless to act effectively when it came to his sons.

Absalom spent years gathering supporters and creating conditions that would allow him to attack and kill his own father and take the throne, but David took no action until he was forced to flee by his son's advancing army. It doesn't seem possible he had not heard of Absalom's conspiracy, and if that is the case it underscores all the more his poor relationship with his children. David's own loyal supporters safeguarded him and gave their lives in warfare against Absalom's men, even though they heard the bewildering command of the king to his generals: "Be gentle with the young man Absalom for my sake." I can imagine their eyes growing wide with the wonder of it. *Be gentle* with a man who had risen up in arms against the God-appointed ruler, his own father? *Be gentle* with the hateful son of a beloved king? It didn't make sense to these fighting men. They were putting their lives on the line to protect the leader they loved, and he wanted them to treat his treacherous son with *gentleness?*

Nevertheless, they obeyed, and as David's superior forces defeated the pretender's army, Joab, David's top commander, took matters into his own hands: he gathered a number of his best men and hunted Absalom down, killing him in spite of the king's order.

I sense that Joab, a hard, no-nonsense soldier, a get-with-the program kind of leader, was disgusted with David's inability to deal properly with his sons. Joab had no sympathy for anything that stood in the way of political necessity. Joab made it his business to be aware of everything, and if David wasn't going to take care of the situation, he would. We who need to be in control of everything often find ourselves feeling we must take matters into our own hands, because no one else wants to, and we are in danger of losing all that truly matters. It's hard to trust God is more interested in our situations than we can imagine.

Joab may have had little respect for laws or commands that got in his way, but he had a heart for the men who were fighting courageously for their king. Like so many military commanders, he loved his men and felt personally any disregard for the hardships they suffered, any rebuffs of their dedication. When word came to David that Absalom had been killed, we read:

The king was shaken. He went up to the room over the gateway and wept. As he went, he said: "O my son Absalom! My son, my son Absalom! If only I had died instead of you—O Absalom, my son, my son!"

Joab was told, "The king is weeping and mourning for Absalom." And for the whole army the victory that day was turned into mourning, because on that day the troops heard it said, "The king is grieving for his son." The men stole into the city that day as men steal in who are ashamed when they flee from battle. The king covered his face and cried aloud, "O my son Absalom! O Absalom, my son, my son!"

Then Joab went into the house to the king and said, "Today you have humiliated all your men, who have just saved your life and the lives of your sons and daughters and the lives of your wives and concubines. You love those who hate you and hate those who love you. You have made it clear today that the commanders and their men mean nothing to you. I see that you would be pleased if Absalom were alive today and all of us were dead. Now go out and encourage your men. I swear by the LORD that if you don't go out, not a man will be left with you by nightfall. This will be worse for you than all the calamities that have come upon you from your youth till now."

So the king got up and took his seat in the gateway. When the men were told, "The king is sitting in the gateway," they all came before him.

—2 Samuel 18:33–19:8

Many was the time after my brother was gone I could have said to my father, "I can see you would be pleased if my brother were alive today and I was dead." Anything I was doing for my father, all of the effort expended, seemed to mean so little. He wanted Danny. He talked about my brother so much as his memory faded; it was clear he wished my brother were still with us so he could take care of him. My father—and my mother, had she survived—would gladly have had my brother alive with all of the accompanying pain and suffering over any other choice.

Every time I came upon those words in 2 Samuel, I could feel the Joab in me. The man told it like it was, and I respect that. Joab was disgusted with the weakness of his leader, and that connected with me. I wanted to appear before my parents and shake some sense into them like Joab did with David, demanding they open their eyes and see they were focusing all their energies on the child who was interested only in what they had to give and were ignoring the child who wanted them to be strong and prudent. They gave away all they had to hold on to my brother but did not call out to me as I left for a distant land.

With Joab's rebuke, David pulled himself together and set aside his grief to minister to those who looked to him for recognition and acknowledgment. He went to the city gate, where nobles and others routinely held court and met with their constituents. His exhausted and mentally defeated troops passed before him, men who should have been celebrating because of their great victory but who saw their defense and protection had caused the king a terrible agony. Joab's harsh words caused David to see that as much as he wanted to seclude himself in grief, others depended upon him, and his refusal to act could be his undoing. He summoned enough of a public face to thank and congratulate his men.

Today my heart feels again the sorrow over the relationship my parents and I could have had, lost forever. How I regret my own inability to see their pain and help them. How I mourn their absence as my wisdom-givers. I can cry until the end of my life and never find the cure I am seeking, for some things are not resolved in this lifetime. We can continue to revisit our unquenchable emotions that smolder within us like coals, and for what? Does it ever provide relief? We so want to know why, to understand the reasons, to be able to make the pieces fit so we can rest with an "Aha! So *that's* why it happened." We keep looking for a moment that will explain it all, heal every hurt, put to rest all frustration. Sometimes there are, simply and with finality, no good reasons for what has happened.

But there will be, someday, an explanation that will fill up the cavities that pain has created. By that time we may find we no longer care. God does not always show us what He is creating, what He is perfecting. We can ruin what He is after by being willing to surrender *only* if we can understand. What comes into our lives may not be His direct will—the Lord does not rub His hands together with delight, proclaiming, "Oh, goodie! Abandonment and starvation! That's what I want for My child!"

But He is able to use it and thwart the enemy. We're not to lay down on the railroad tracks and allow evil, disappointment, frustration, and regret to run over us like a locomotive, but neither are we to spend the rest of our lives pounding away at the injustice of life, because then we truly have allowed Satan access to the most vulnerable parts of us.

I surrender even though I don't understand it all. I'm tired of trying to figure out what my parents were thinking, tired of trying to fathom things that are unfathomable. I'm exhausted from carrying my own burden of being someone who knows better, thinks better, *is* better. I'm not better! But this structure I've created to live in has a life of its own, and I keep acting in accordance with its dictates. Is there a way to just *stop*?

M. Scott Peck, in his book *People of the Lie*, wrote about a patient who, after much psychoanalytic therapy, had a dream of a lovely machine she had constructed. It was packed with defensive weapons and shined to perfection. In her dream, her machine was guaranteed to be the winning factor in a war in which she was involved, and she was extremely proud of it. Peck questioned his client about the dream and finally suggested the machine represented her need to protect her sense of who she was. He was already aware she could not admit she secretly loved the behaviors she claimed she wanted to be rid of. He had come to see she had no interest in combating any of the thinking that had plunged her into trouble time and time again, and he wondered about her reasons for entering therapy. Neither he, nor any knowledge presented to her, was going to cause her to give up the self she had constructed. Now she came to him with a dream that had such strong symbolism it was hard to miss. What were all those elaborate weapons really for?

He reasoned the machine of her dream was her own internal hardware used to protect herself from change, from healthy thinking and relationships, and she reacted vehemently. Surprised, he asked her why she disagreed.

"'Because it was beautiful,' Charlene wailed. She went on, almost crooning to the image of the machine. 'My machine was a thing of beauty. It was intricate. It was intricate beyond belief. It could do so many things. It had been constructed with such care and ingenuity. It had so many levels and operations. It was a masterpiece of engineering. . . . It was the most beautiful thing ever made.' "[1] As she spoke, Peck understood unequivocally how Charlene had created her defenses and would never let them go because they were an integral part of her. She would never get free because it would require her to remove herself from her beautiful machine and leave it behind.

Everyone uses something to protect emotional wounds. The imagery of self-defense may not come out so vividly in our dreams, but the fact that it exists comes out in our behavior in some way. We lend a lot of strength to our illusions about ourselves, seeing in the mirror the reflection of victims or abandoned children or self-made conquerors; the illusion can take many forms. Whatever the fantasy, we choose to construct elaborate patterns of thought and action, or to do the simplest of wrongheaded things just to make sure we don't get pounded again on that open sore. We might be aware of what we're doing or we could be unable to face the truth about ourselves just now. But the Lord is always working to get through, to speak to us in the midst of our machinery, and He is tireless. He will never stop trying to get a foot in the door, whether He speaks to us in dreams or through friends and counselors or in the depleting heat of the crucible.

All I have constructed to protect myself must be brought to the cross, where Jesus can give me a vision of my own slavery: my slavery to my need to be loved and appreciated, my need to be special, my need to be right, to be better. My machine may be a thing of beauty, but what a hideous beauty. It provides me no hope. Its intricacies keep me running, even when I am drained. I don't control it; it controls me, and it takes every ounce of energy to keep it shined and on display. There's no purpose to it anymore. It's a burden, a terrible burden, and I want to be free.

If I don't listen to the Joab of my Spirit-filled conscience, if I'm not even interested in training myself to listen, it will be worse for me than all the calamities that have come upon me from my youth until now.

— Chapter Twelve —

Climbing the Mountain of Forgiveness

We are not converted only once in our lives but many times, and this endless series of large and small conversions, inner revolutions, leads to our transformation in Christ. But while we may have the generosity to undergo one or two such upheavals, we cannot face the necessity of further and greater rendings of our inner self, without which we cannot finally become free.

—THOMAS MERTON[1]

Years ago, my husband and I tackled a partial climb up Mount Washington in New Hampshire. We had done this on our first date more than a decade before, and I remembered it as a challenging but fun workout. We began our hike with confidence. The hiking trail on Mount Washington starts out as a beaten path but gradually becomes a steeper climb over larger and more numerous rocks and boulders. After what seemed like hours of constant climbing I began to tire, and when I get tired, I get very cranky. "Almost there," Larry encouraged me. "Let's not give up!"

We were dripping with sweat and he matched my slow pace as I willed my legs to keep climbing. I could see a turn up ahead and hoped for a small landing where we could walk on flat ground, even if just for a few minutes. But no. We made the turn and I looked up to see a long column of rock. More rock! Harder climbing! I was so discouraged I fought back tears.

This happened again, and then again, and yes—again! We'd stand at the turn and all my hopes would be dashed and I would cry out, "No! I can't do it!" Larry urged me on. "Come on, honey. It's not that much farther. You can do it." People were passing by like speeding cars, or at least that's how they seemed to me. I felt like a rhinoceros in a herd of gazelles.

Two hours of increasingly difficult ascent made me so exhausted that by the time we reached the rest area, I thought I would pass out. While I lay on a picnic table in the sun, depleted of all energy, Larry spread a little feast for us. He handed me a sandwich and I found the strength to take a bite.

Like a dry plant sucking up water, energy soon flowed into me. I felt it start in my head and spread to my arms and hands, and then my legs, until I was sitting up and eating that sandwich as though it were life itself (which it was at that moment!). I finished it off with a banana and sat there marveling at how just a few minutes before I had been sure I would have to be carried back down the mountain. I was still tired, but it wasn't the weak, dried-up weariness of just a half hour before.

We still laugh about that climb, and I insist to friends it was like two nonstop hours on a Stairmaster. I remember how hard it was, but guess what? I would do it again. The next time I'd be more prepared, of course. I'd stop and rest more along the way, bring snacks to fortify me. I'd develop my climbing muscles before tackling the hike again. And I'd remember no matter how many turns reveal yet another long climb, there really *is* a place to rest up ahead.

I've been on the trek up the Mount Washington of my development. It has been arduous at times and I have sat down in the middle of the path in complete dejection and wept with the exertion of it. Just when I have a little hope I might be nearing the end of the climb, I turn a corner in my mind and happen upon a memory, and the same old stuff I thought I'd passed way behind inclines before me like a big, snickering joke, filled with a life of its own and mocking that I dared expect it to be over. What do I do with all of the truth of the matter, lying there in front of me—all of the ugly memories, all of the painful emotions that capture me when I return to an evocative moment?

Some people teach we are never to return to such memories, or we are to consecrate the memories by imagining Jesus at the scene. I have no formula. I am in favor of whatever works to help us forgive. But this does not mean we *forget*. Our world has been so affected by the use of computers we frequently compare our brains to them as though the two are exactly alike. There is a generally held belief our minds are like a hard drive on which our memories are recorded indelibly. We suppose we can access memories and they will be accurate, unaltered, true. If this were so, forgiveness should mean we could simply erase memories of how we've been hurt, and the offenses would be gone. But our brains are far more complex than computers. While it can be helpful to explain memories and ideas with technological metaphors, we are not big pieces of hardware with a bunch of chips inserted. Using another metaphor, we cannot rewind the videotape of memory and forgive another by erasing an offense, and then fast-forward and erase future temptations to remember.

There are times upon the mountain when Jesus shows Himself in His glory. In those moments, we feel like we can lay down everything that hinders us and separates us from our relationship with Him. But the path continues, and the same old fallout from life's past battles tries to pull us back to the place of transgression. We wonder if our character was truly touched by our mountaintop experience. There, we felt compelled to place our angers and wants under the radiant heat of God's presence, and it wasn't hard to do at all. Back on the climb of everyday life, we find ourselves dwelling on those same angers and wants that rise up and discourage us once again. We wish we could look at our situation without the emotion it has been connected with all these years, just be able to view it and the people involved without letting it rip us apart.

The Lord wants to cleanse us. We don't have to live in that place where memories grip us, hold on to us, shake us like a floppy toy in a dog's mouth. Something *has* happened to us. But our hearts are unable to plug in to the Father and find peace when we are wedded to judgments and bitter evaluations of those who hurt us. We are reluctant to shed them and move on. They still define us, and we can't yet see we love them more than we love God. Ultimately, it is all about who and what we love.

"Love" describes that to which we give our strength, our hearts, our thoughts, our energies. What we're holding on to takes all we've got. In our fallen state we are inclined to love our sin and hate God. Because our hearts are full of these matters, we see inaccurately. We shuffle our way in the darkness of wrong thinking. "No one is ever united with Jesus Christ," said Oswald Chambers, "until he is willing to relinquish not sin only, but his whole way of looking at things."[2]

I knew from the moment I met the Lord Jesus Christ I could not leave my judgments about others locked up in a safe deposit box inside my head. Every single time I read the words of Jesus in Mark 11:25-26, I knew what I was doing. "And when you stand praying, if you hold anything against anyone, forgive him, so that your Father in heaven may forgive you your sins." I could not relinquish my personal inventory of rights and demands. They were all I had! But I knew if the words of Jesus were true, my own sins could not be forgiven until I forgave each member of my family. I was not unaware of my sin. I was persistently aware and felt helpless. I prayed my burden of anger would be lifted from me miraculously, because I had no power to lift it from myself.

I haven't taken a poll, but I wouldn't be surprised if unforgiveness is the biggest obstruction most of us face. Our very nature wants to hold on to hurt and find vindication and acceptance in some final display we think will move the mountain inside of us. But Jesus did not say the mountain was moved by someone else's action; the mountain is moved by *our* action. We must speak to the mountain of unforgiveness and, when we pray, actively forgive.

How do we do that when we have a lifetime of offenses built up in our souls? I think we start by *beginning* to forgive. We must take the first step and then continue to forgive, over and over, until full forgiveness is present. "Believe that you have received it," said Jesus. When someone with whom I am angry surfaces before me when I am praying, I speak to that mountain: "Father, I forgive him. Lord, I forgive her. Even if he knew what he was doing, even if she is filled with hatred and evil, I forgive as You forgave." I pray for that person in the best way I know how. Sometimes it's easier to do than other times. Some people have simply gotten on my wrong side or hurt my feelings, and it's a little easier to give up my right to be angry when the offense hasn't cut too deep. It's when the perpetrator of hurtful things has sliced to the bone, perhaps repeatedly, that I must call upon the Lord's help to pray for him or her. I don't always know how to pray for someone to receive God's blessing if he or she participates in evil deeds. Some people seem to enjoy perpetrating evil. I remember, though, that the Lord often blesses by sending us through difficult passages in order to bring us to the end of our abilities, and so I pray God will bless the person with *exactly* the blessing he or she needs—one that may include some very hard lessons. I pray He will draw that person to Himself.

There is not something wrong with me if I can't *feel* forgiving. It can take a great deal of time, sometimes even years, to come to a place of complete forgiveness. It is a process. It is not an instantaneous occurrence unless God does a miracle, which is, of course, welcome. But no matter how I feel, I stand on that forgiveness. Someday the feelings will catch up. Forgiving is an action I choose to do despite my feelings.

John and Paula Sandford say, "Hopefully, every man will be so wounded some time that he will come upon the happy discovery that no man can forgive anybody anything at any time! We actually think we are pretty good fellows, and sometimes say, 'Forgiving was always easy for me. I never could hold a grudge.' There goes a self-deluded man. Forgiveness is never easy for any man. And no man can ever forgive another. Forgiveness is an impossibility for human flesh. The mind can fool itself, and outwardly gracious people can think they really are that way, but 'the heart is deceitful above all things, and desperately wicked' (Jeremiah 17:9), and no man is capable of forgiveness. . . . We simply receive by faith that Jesus has accomplished it for us."[3]

Forgiveness *is* an impossibility through our own will. But Jesus has given us a new heart, cleansed and desiring to be like Him, with power to do something we could not do on our own.

We've got His Spirit within us now, and "the law of the Spirit of life set me free from the law of sin and death" (Romans 8:2). Yes, the unforgiveness will surface again. It does not go without a fight! But our weapons are not willpower or strength of character or intelligence or a laid-back personality—none of those things will fight our feelings of being horribly, agonizingly wronged.

I have pondered the parable of the prodigal son, imagining how it might end. Is the older son able to take his father's hand

and walk with him to the house? Did the father know his son felt the way he did? What father would not be shocked his compliant and dutiful son spat out years of venomous pain in words that implied he felt treated as nothing more than a slave? The younger son had just thrown himself upon the father, professing his unworthiness and begging to be treated as a hired hand, and here was his older son, spitefully pushing him away and claiming he had been treated with indifference.

I wonder if the father reeled with emotion. He had spent months or years in worry over the younger son, looking out over the land, hoping to see the distant figure of his reckless child upon the horizon. Day after day, there had been no word of him. Night after night, he must have lain awake, praying his son was safe and would find his way home somehow. Finally, his prayers were answered, and the regret and fear and anger of the past were forgotten in the moment of elation and pity when his lost son knelt before him, seeking forgiveness.

The father's joy set off hours of preparation for a feast. Think of how long it must have taken to slaughter a calf and cook it! Workers must have scurried to engage musicians and break out wine. Bread would be baked, fruit and cheese brought out as messengers were sent to surrounding houses inviting friends and family to a celebration. The returning son would have been given over to the charge of servants who would clean him up, dress his wounds, and massage his calloused feet. The robe of honor would be cleaned and the ring of family identity would be shined to a sparkle. In my mind, the son had to have returned in the morning because this was an entire day's work. Maybe the father had made a habit of going outside in the midmorning before the day became too hot, watching the road as he prayed, and it was during this time he saw his son make the turn onto the lane leading to the house.

The older son enters the story as he is coming from work. The sun might have begun to set, and in the distance he would have seen the dwelling ablaze with activity and heard the sound of dancing and happy music, something not heard in his father's house for a long time.

He must have seen family servants running errands, laughing at the great change that had come over the estate. He called to one of them, the parable tells us, asking what was going on, and we can hear the lighthearted reply of the man, telling the older brother his father had killed the fattened calf because he had his son back "safe and sound." In that moment, the older son's heart was gripped with . . . what? Shock? Sadness? The Bible tells us "he became angry," and I infer that anger may not have been the first emotion that arose. He *became* angry—arriving there after traversing the feelings that raced through him. He might even have been sincerely happy for a moment, but he could not remain there.

Whatever stirred in his gut as he viewed the scene before him, it was too much for him. He could not take another step closer to the sounds of merrymaking when his own heart was so heavy. I see him finding a place to sit as he looks at the house, meditating on all that has happened, wondering if his father has even noticed he had never asked for anything—not for the inheritance he had received, not for a party, not for anything that might cause the father greater agony or concern. He knew the relentless sorrow that had filled the house since his brother left. He knew the turmoil his younger brother's behavior had generated throughout their years growing up together. It's possible he sat remembering incident after incident, argument after angry argument, cataloging without effort the seasons of discontent and disruption in the life of his family. I can imagine that on the day his brother left for the distant country he thought to himself, "At least now there will be some peace and quiet." He found the peace and quiet was accompanied by dull isolation. His brother's absence did not allow him to be seen. He was invisible when his brother was present and also when he was not.

When did the father discover his older son was not at the party? Was it dark outside? Could it have come to him suddenly that in all the commotion, he hadn't even thought to send word to the older son that his younger brother was alive and had come home? Maybe he had grabbed a servant and asked if there were any signs of the older son and been told yes, he was sitting on the other side of the road, and had been there for some time. "I asked him when he was coming in," the servant might have relayed to the father, "and he told me he wasn't planning on it anytime soon."

Jesus tells His listeners the father went out and pleaded with his son. Pleaded! This is a word that connotes supplication, but also offering reasons for or against something. The *American Heritage Dictionary* says as it refers to law, "plead" means "to present as an answer to a charge, an indictment, or a declaration made against one."

As I read the parable, I see the father walking across the road and sitting down next to his son. He begins to plead his case. Perhaps he told his son of all the dreams he'd had as a young father, how proud he had been on the day the oldest son, his firstborn came into the world. All of the hopes he'd had for his boys. He had not meant to neglect the older boy, but time got away from him and the younger son seemed to require more of him. "You were always so strong, so capable," the father might have disclosed, "not like your brother."

In spite of all of the indignation I felt, I so wanted to forgive my brother and my parents. As a Christian I knew I should, and my failure weighed upon me heavily. But how does one forgive without the acknowledgment of offense? It fed the cisterns of anger within me that no one in my family could bring themselves to ask, "Will you forgive me?"

It feels impossible to give up that anger whether you are the sibling of a drug-addicted child, the child of an alcoholic parent, a woman sexually abused, a man with a cruel and heartless father. The anger flows forth, coating every surface of our hearts like a sticky sap. It becomes so much a part of us we don't know how to scrape it off the walls of our identity. For so many years, my anger fueled me, energized me. Anger gave me determination and purpose, and it seems indestructible. Just when you think you've confessed it and left it at the altar—this time, you've laid it down for good—it pops up like a submarine on an emergency blow to the surface.

That's why I understand the son's reaction to the father's plea. It's at this point, when the father has laid out his heart, entreating his son to see how he regrets the distance between them, the son hurls his accusations at the father. He had listened to the plea. He heard the supplication. But his anger had to have its release before the father whose affection he craved. When the moment of self-justification arrives, the moment when we testify to all of the injuries of the past, it's as though we must bring the object of our desire to its knees. We must cause it the pain it caused us. We must punish it with the last gasp of our bitter provocation. That's the moment we need to be heard. That's the moment when most people react to the cry of the wounded with defensiveness.

But not the father in our parable. He received his son's spleen-venting rebuke and ceased his plea. But do you see the father did not reprimand his son? He did not try to defend himself, did not cry out, "You're wrong, you don't understand!" This wise father knew the pressure had found its release. The truth is many people who are angry truly *do* want to forgive and be forgiven themselves. They want to discharge all of the malignant feelings, free themselves of the burden, because carrying it is exhausting. We need a moment of vulnerability, of honesty, where we meet face-to-face with the one we've judged and hear their pain is as great as ours, and we can embrace each other in absolution and mercy.

There's something powerful about the question, "Will you forgive me?" It's a defenseless question, different from "I'm sorry." "Will you forgive me?" requires an answer, knowing the response might well be, "No." The words "I'm sorry" require nothing. Even when heartfelt, they can be thrown down in haste or used as a shield: "I said I was sorry! What more do you want?"

Sometimes "I'm sorry" sends a burst of oxygen to the flames of anger, because it asks us once again to bear a burden instead of being offered the opportunity to lay it down. We feel compelled to say, "Oh, that's okay," when we really don't want to, and the matter is unresolved.

"Will you forgive me?" places the requestor in a position of weakness. We are in the tense opening between mercy and exile as we await the response. For some folks, the thought of being pushed away is too frightening to contemplate, and they refuse the opportunity for cleansing.

I think of my brother, who had no ability to control himself, who was directionless, who had no internal scale on which to weigh the decisions he made. I think of my mother, wanting so much to make things right but without the strength to look fearlessly at truth because it might reveal she was wrong, and that would have withered her. I think of my father, stubborn and passive and frightened all at the same time, convinced if he remained very still, everything would be okay.

Who will come and plead with me? My brother is gone. My mother is gone. My father, even when he was alive, was gone, his cave of protection having taken him prisoner. I will never have the opportunity to look them in the eyes as they ask, "Will you forgive me?" They have no one to send to plead their case with me.

And so I must plead it for them. They have no advocate. I can ask the Lord for insight into the heart of my family and plead on their behalf. I know their weaknesses. I know their reasoning. I know what they would say if they could, if they'd had the ability, if they'd understood the necessity of it.

I will plead their case with me, because it is the only way I can prepare myself to be found and brought home. God can give us insight into the pain and loneliness our families experienced. He can show us what we were not able to see when we sat in the middle of the confusing tangle of family crises. He can reveal to us the confessions our siblings could not express, the vulnerabilities our mothers were afraid to reveal, the inadequacies our fathers could not bring themselves to describe.

I will plead their case, because I know them and I love them. I can hear the voice of my mother as she explains to me how frightened she was. She tells me of her terror as she spent sleepless nights wondering irrationally if she had been responsible for passing on some gene of addiction to her son because her father was a violent alcoholic, afraid if she didn't try to make amends to Danny for this terrible evil she had placed upon him she would never know reprieve. I can hear my father break down as he tells me he just didn't know what to do, reeling from the hurt of a child who rejected his love and could never be comforted, trying to be stronger but finding nothing worked. I can hear my parents tell me they were hindered in seeking help by their generation's attitudes and their own family upbringing.

I can hear my brother tell me he doesn't know why he can't control himself. He's ashamed he's so difficult. He doesn't understand why he feels so angry all the time. He just knows he never felt right and the only thing that would give him relief from the incessant agitation was drugs or alcohol or both. He tells me he never felt he could live up to the standard I set. I plead their cases to myself, and I ask, "Will you forgive them?"

"Forgiveness breaks the cycle of blame and loosens the stranglehold of guilt," says Philip Yancey. "It accomplishes these two things through a remarkable linkage, placing the forgiver on the same side as the party who did the wrong."[4] I can call upon the love the Holy Spirit has shed abroad in my heart to show me the lost and struggling souls He knows so well, and I can say, "I forgive them."

Jesus said we are to forgive "seventy times seven" (Matthew 18:22). I forgive, and then I must forgive *again*, each time the feelings assault me and demand an audience. As I said before, we cannot "forgive and forget," a cliché that appears nowhere in the Bible and has burdened millions of believers with the erroneous belief we have not forgiven until we've forgotten. How wonderful if we could forget! It would be far easier than forgiving. Forgiving is hard work. Forgiving means knowing, acknowledging, seeing plainly, standing in the light, seeing the evil, seeing the carelessness, the thoughtlessness, the cruelty, and yet refusing to testify against the people who offended us. Forgiveness is an ongoing process. We are set free from those binding cords so that we might forgive as many times as necessary to get the message to the heart that there is no value in pursuing the pain. God asks me to trust Him, to continue to cut the cords and offer my answer over and over: "I forgive."

It seems to me my bitterness and hate through the years should have disqualified me from receiving the strength to do these things, but no—God wants to help me. Philip Yancey writes, "Grace comes free of charge to people who do not deserve it and I am one of those people. I think back to who I was— resentful, wound tight with anger, a single hardened link in a long chain of ungrace learned from family and church. Now I am trying in my own small way to pipe to the tune of grace. I do so because I know, more surely than I know anything, that any pang of healing or forgiveness or goodness I have ever felt comes solely from the grace of God."[5]

Unforgiveness isn't our only challenge, to be sure, but somehow it seems to emerge as the root of so many other problems. So the Holy Spirit must drill down into the rock of our personalities and insert the probe that will expose these sometimes forgotten, sometimes unacknowledged deep motivations. If we confess our sins, God is faithful, He's just, He's truthful, and we will be forgiven. He has no desire to harm us. It is His love that brings truth. When He urges us farther up the mountain, it is because He loves us. He will give us breathers, times of refreshing, so the work can be done without harm to our hearts and minds. He will continue to walk with us, and we will sense Him more deeply.

Having made it to the summit, I realize all the bitter feelings that empowered me before were not productive. I lost energy quickly and found myself in despair, but now that I've received sustenance—the comfort and mercy of God's Word to me—I am ready for the next climb. It's not that the hike will be easier now that I've done it once; in fact, it might be more challenging! But I don't view those boulders in the same way. They're still there, but I'm prepared. I've exercised my ability to climb over them, and they are no longer obstacles in my way but steps to the next high place where I can look back and see the distance I have traveled by the grace of God.

— CHAPTER THIRTEEN —

Standing on the Summit

Our yesterdays present irreparable things to us; it is true that we have lost opportunities which will never return, but God can transform this destructive anxiety into a constructive thoughtfulness for the future. Let the past sleep, but let it sleep on the bosom of Christ. Leave the Irreparable Past in His hands, and step out into the Irresistible Future with Him.

—OSWALD CHAMBERS[1]

Most people read the story of the lost son and are moved by the tremendous emotion of a father and son reunited by the son's acknowledgment of his guilt. They read the story and identify with the son who has come to his senses and realized what a muddle he has made of his life, who swallows hard and makes the long walk to his father's door—but on the way is nearly accosted by his father, who has raced from his lookout to throw his arms around the son for whom he has prayed, most likely pacing the floor late at night in the parental agony of waiting.

Few who read the story are willing to admit it's the older son that most describes them. It's the older son's bitterness, his fulminating anger, that makes a connection deep within, igniting afresh the memory of parents who ran after the child who consistently flayed them with disobedience and disrespect. Oh, how we know the older brother's spiteful cry: "I slaved all these years for you, and you never threw a party for me!"

Why couldn't he see his father's love? Was he not close enough to his father to know he was loved? He didn't feel comfortable asking for what belonged to him and perhaps wasn't sure it did. How did this happen? Did the son move far away, or had the father let a wall build between them? Or had they both missed each other so massively they couldn't meet on any level except a superficial one? The older son was waiting for his father to show his love by offering it to him. In his mind, this was his requirement: If the father really loved him, he'd acknowledge the sacrifice and commitment he'd made. It wasn't the party thrown for the younger brother that made him jealous. It was the acknowledgment. His brother was being celebrated for . . . *what*? He hadn't done anything, he hadn't sacrificed anything, he hadn't shown his love by dutiful obedience. He was a wasteful, arrogant, thoughtless human being and he got a *party* thrown for him. "I've been with you all these years," said the older brother with incredulity, "and you never offered a feast for me and my friends."

The older son had apparently missed the significance of his father giving him his grand portion of the inheritance. So the father pleads with him. His heart is softened, touched with the truth of enduring love, and his eyes are opened to see what he could not see before. He is cherished.

I see it all now, or at least what I think is all. I turn around from my vantage point of age and maturity and experience, and I look back upon my family's life. I stand with my Father, high upon the mountain of His dwelling place, and I draw strength from Him as I hold His hand and gaze upon the sad mess in which I grew up. I know I have been brought to a place of acceptance because I can watch all of the memories as they parade before us, and I recognize the suffering within them, but I am no longer filled with the awful pain of offense. I was once the older brother who stood outside the house, shouting at the father and mother I could not forgive, unable to enter the house while my younger brother was being celebrated for what I saw as a pathetic spectacle of hope—hope he would reform, hope he would not spit in their faces and run off again, hope that this time, it would be different. But now I am the blessed child of God who recognizes the depths to which I myself had fallen. I had become hard and had sunk like granite in the river of life. My Lord reached His long arm of deliverance into that water and drew me out, and as He grasped my heart of stone it turned to a heart of flesh and I was released. I have given myself to Him forever. "I run in the path of your commands, for you have set my heart free" (Psalm 119:32).

My Father's outstretched hand has drawn me to this place where I can view it all with peace. It had its work. A. W. Tozer wrote, "There must be a work of God in destruction before we are set free. We must invite the cross to do its deadly work within us. . . . The cross is rough, and it is deadly, but it is effective. There comes a moment when its work is finished and the suffering victim dies. After that is resurrection glory and power, and the pain is forgotten for joy that the veil is taken away and we have entered in actual spiritual experience the Presence of the living

God."[2] My memories are simply that—memories. They have no power over me, and they can no longer hold me in a place of pain and sensitivity.

To be able to forgive my family has changed all of my relationships. I don't mean I act radically different than I did before or that anyone can necessarily tell I have exchanged bad blood for good. I am very aware, though, of how unforgiveness rested upon my heart like . . . well, like a dead body. Paul said in Romans, in its original intent, "Who will deliver me from this corpse?" I comprehend that cry. Unforgiveness was a dead weight inside, dragged around for so many years I thought its heavy spiritual poundage was a fundamental part of me. "Thanks be to God," he continued, explaining he was delivered only "through Jesus Christ our Lord" (Romans 7:24-25). Only Jesus could give me the power to stop drinking poison every day of my life, for that is what unforgiveness is. It is toxic. There's no drug test for unforgiveness, but it is as deadly as arsenic.

That one concentrated stream of unforgiveness has been broken, and I have been amazed at the emancipation it has wrought. I can rest more confidently in the knowledge God loves me. I know I am flawed and yet He continues to love me tenderly. I know He is going to work His plans and purposes in my life in spite of my inadequacies and failures, simply because I am His and am called by His name. Sometimes I fall back into that old interior refrain, "Why is everyone more important than I am, Lord?" But it can't persist. The Lord has taken me in and carried me, attended to me, provided for me, urged me on, motivated me, steadied me. I have not been alone on this journey, and He will never leave me.

Once many years ago, I was visiting friends and settled in front of their fireplace to pray while they were at work. I found a comfortable position and began talking with the Lord. "Father, I trust You. My life is in Your hands. I trust You to lead me and guide me. Precious Lord, I trust You."

Deep inside my head, I heard a very quiet voice: "Liar."

It was so distinct—almost audible—that I sat for a moment, startled. I thought about what I had been saying when I heard it, and I said aloud, "Satan, I am not a liar. *You* are the liar! Get lost!"

Having dispatched my accuser, I began praying again. "Lord Jesus, I trust You to take care of me. I thank You for walking with me, for going ahead of me and making my paths straight. I trust You to show me where to go."

Soft but insistent, it came again. "Liar."

Now I was a bit irritated, and I called out, "Satan, I resist you!" But that quiet little voice spoke again, and I heard it clearly: "Sue, it's not the devil. It's Me."

Stunned, I sat with my mouth open, listening intently. "You don't trust Me, Sue," He whispered. "You don't know *how* to trust Me. You're not really sure of what trust *is*. You're not fooling Me with your nice words. Let's be real with each other. You know you don't trust Me." He was so gentle, and I felt no disapproval or condemnation. He was simply stating the facts and inviting me to respond.

I was stung. I wanted to say, "That's not true, Lord! Of course I trust You! I've been walking with You for nearly two decades, I believe Your Word, I followed Your call into ministry, I've preached Your Word, I have devoted everything to You!" But I knew better than to argue with the Master of the Universe. There was no point in telling the Almighty He was wrong about me.

I stopped my gathering protest and thought about it. Did I really trust the Lord? I considered recent moments of crisis, both big and small, and as my mind touched on various events, it came inevitably to the struggle I'd had with my family situation for so many years. My defenses slowly withered, and I was finally silent inside. "Let's be real with each other," He had said.

"All right, Lord," I responded, my head bowed as I spoke out loud. "You want to be real? I'll be real. No, I don't trust You. I *can't* trust You. I have dedicated my life to You, but You don't help me. I serve You but You don't rescue me. Remember a couple of months ago when I was short on my rent money? Where were You? And last year when the phone bill was so large because I had been on the road and had to make so many long distance calls—where were You when that bill came due and I had to scramble to find a way to pay it?"

"Where have you been when money's been tight? Why haven't you alerted me to whatever it is that causes friends to reject me? Why am I always struggling with my weight, my finances, my emotions? Why can't I figure out what I'm supposed to do?"

From the shallow edge of superficial complaints I fell off into my deep ocean of grievances. Now I was sobbing, and all my heartache rolled out. "My family, my family! Why can't my mother be proud of me? Why can't my father take action? Why am I so alone? Where are You when I need You, Lord? Why have I always had to hack my way through the jungle alone? It's so much work, and I feel like You stand back with your arms folded, watching me pound away with a machete, just trying to make a way in the jungle. You're right, Lord," I wailed, "I don't trust You! How can I trust You when *You never help me?*"

Expecting a harsh rebuke, I heard the merciful reply as I wept. "Ah, now we have the truth," He said. "Now that you have been honest, we can work together. Even though you aren't able to see it, I helped you find the rent money and pay your phone bill. I supply your needs—you can't see My hand in it right now because you've judged Me as withholding, but it's there. I know how alone you feel, but I've been with you from the beginning; you aren't mature enough yet to sense My presence. You aren't making your way through this jungle alone." As I sat with my eyes closed, concentrating on His voice, I envisioned myself hacking through tropical growth with a machete—but it was only the little bit left after a Divine Hand had cleared the way before me. I could have strolled through the path left open, but instead I thrashed at tendrils of vines as though they were trees, with the force of a lumberjack swinging an axe. I had to giggle at the comedy of it. We really do see what we want to see, and since I chose to see my way as hard, I worked like it was instead of resting in what had already been done for me.

"Hate blinds the eyes," write the Sandfords, who tell us that "our hatred of fellow human beings colors what we see of God— or prevents it altogether; we do not love or see God. That is one of the primary facts which necessitate continual conversion of the heart. Our hidden and forgotten judgments, especially against our fathers and mothers, prevent us from seeing God as He is."[3] I could not see God accurately because of the sludge in my soul, the waiting-to-be-cleaned-out hollows of my thinking. My mind needed renewal, and the Lord was beginning the more penetrating aspects of that work. In the years following that encounter with the Father, He revealed the awful indictments I'd made about my family. He showed me the arrogant conclusions I had reached. He laid bare the awful motivations I carried to defend and vindicate myself. He pulled me into the light with relentless compassion. He wasn't about to leave me as I was because He knew what I could be. It took a long time to bring me to the place where I could stand on this particular mountain with Him after forgiving my family, but the trip was worth it.

I am able now to let offenses go in a way I was not able to before. It's almost analogous to riding a bicycle: once you learn how, it's just a matter of getting on the thing and peddling! Because the light broke through and showed me the way to forgiveness, I know that way now, forever, and if I do not walk that way it is nobody's fault but my own. I am convinced with unwavering certainty I must go to the cross with every bitter judgment, irritation, and angry response. I can forgive only because He lives in me.

Like someone released from years of prison, I don't want to go back there ever again, and so I must always be on the lookout for the entrance of the dangerous thoughts and feelings that could grip me once again, if given the chance. The enemy is fond of insinuating I have not forgiven because I occasionally get a whiff of the aroma of my past. Before he died, my father and I had conversations that would once have made me apoplectic with frustration. Because of the work within, I found myself thinking, "Is it worth it? Have you truly forgiven?" I could decide, "Yes, I have," and drop it. That was not possible before. I was not able to decide; my emotions had a power that I let carry me where I did not intend to go.

I'm also supremely grateful I did tell my parents how much I loved them. Thank God! He didn't let me give away that opportunity. I truly believed, still believe, as I did in that moment in the car with my mother as she mustered all of her courage to give me the facts of my birth, I was a loved and wanted child. What else does adoption say if not, "I want *that* one!" There is still room for cleansing, and always will be. It's the work of our lives. I don't always feel magnanimous and benevolent in regard to my family. Frequently, I am irritated yet again when I am reminded of incidents from my past. Sometimes I even fume a bit. But I have the agency and the freedom now to tip my hat to tough things without setting up a base camp at the foot of that mountain and living there for years.

I remember what it felt like to climb every single aspect of that mountain. How well I know each foothold and craggy resting place! It holds no obsessive interest for me anymore: I am done with it. There are better, more productive mountains to scale these days. In another way of explaining it, I used to cheat on my diet(s) and decide, "I've ruined everything!" I sabotaged myself by believing that one infraction meant cancellation of all of the good that had been achieved and there was no way I could begin again. In just the same way, we can recognize a familiar emotional sensation and fear we fooled ourselves when we thought we were free. We *are* free! When I splurge in a momentary weakness, I go right back to the effective eating habits that have become my way of life and chalk up my failures to human nature, determined to bring my frailties to the Light. He will show me what He is working on. I must stand on what I know has been accomplished and proclaim emancipation to my mind, which would love to feast on doubt and have me guilt-ridden and defeated.

"Above all else, guard your heart, for it is the wellspring of life. Put away perversity from your mouth; keep corrupt talk far from your lips. Let your eyes look straight ahead, fix your gaze directly before you. Make level paths for your feet and take only ways that are firm. Do not swerve to the right or the left; keep your foot from evil" (Proverbs 4:23-27). How important it is to guard the heart. How important it is to keep ourselves from swerving to the right or to the left, where we can sideline ourselves in subjugation to the past, to fear, to anger. We must stand as a guard and proclaim to our soul that we will not walk down that path again. "So if the Son sets you free, you will be free indeed" (John 8:36). If we stumble, we must remind ourselves we now walk on a path that is straight and firm. Eventually, our minds will accept the decisions we have made and conform to the new life we've received without fighting us for control.

I find I am not so critical. I'm critical by nature so that's a funny thing for me to say, but what I mean is I recognize hateful judgment when it tries to inflate inside of me, and because I walk in the light, I see it and deal with it. I'm not in the dark when it comes to my own motivations and internal influences. I can keep watch on these things and prevent them from entering and becoming the twisted knot they once tied inside of me. Some days I'm more successful than others, but I am so grateful for the ability to see clearly that this is an area on which I will focus for the rest of my life. "Forgive," I tell myself regularly. When I'm irritated by a grocery store clerk, when a colleague treats me with disrespect, when my husband hits a period of inflexibility, I remind myself: "Forgive." Forgive even when they know what they are doing. Forgive because they are broken, just like I was and am. Forgive because my brokenness has been swallowed up in the triumph of my Savior's sacrifice.

This means I must also continue to forgive my parents and my brother, even though they are all gone. I wish I had been gentle with my mother, who wanted so much to be my friend and share intimacies. I weep sometimes at my arrogance and intolerance of her. I know she knows now what was going on between us, but I regret what I let slip away.

As the ravages of Alzheimer's disease overtook my father, he went on and on about my brother, rehashing the worst things done as though they were treasures of his existence, oblivious to any pain they caused me. Many times, it seemed as though I were his therapist instead of his daughter. I felt like I didn't know him.

And yet I loved him, still love him, and I honor his memory. I thank God he came to the house of a woman in Charleston, West Virginia so many years ago and lost his heart to a tiny baby who had been left behind with no one to value her. No matter what life experiences came between us, I honor him for following his heart. I realize this was all he ever did—follow his heart—and feel pity for the corrosion that heart suffered somewhere in life so his decisions rarely bore good fruit.

Henri Nouwen put it just right: "The return to the 'Father from whom all fatherhood takes its name' allows me to let my dad be no less than the good, loving, but limited human being he is, and to let my heavenly Father be the God whose unlimited, unconditional love melts away all resentments and anger and makes me free to love beyond the need to please or find approval."[4] I'm not waiting for my dad to see me now, or my mother, because I know my heavenly Father sees, and I am content.

A friend once said to me, "Sue, you are the most mentally healthy person I know!" I laughed when she said it because I know my struggles and how easy it is to appear to have it together when inside, some things are calcifying more rapidly than my ability to chase them down and hose them off. But I also marvel someone can see something I can't, that the effect of God's work on my life is visible in some way, and I am grateful, so grateful. Because I love the life God has given me. I am not always happy, but I do not expect to be. I am not always in control, but I know that's not possible, and sometimes I'm ordered to relinquish it and God gives me power to do it. I have occasional rough patches in my marriage, but I can hang on and say, "This too shall pass." I've learned to praise God in all things, and once in a while I delight in the fact I can say with Paul, "I have learned to be content whatever the circumstances. I know what it is to be in need, and I know what it is to have plenty. I have learned the secret of being content in any and every situation, whether well fed or hungry, whether living in plenty or in want. I can do everything through him who gives me strength" (Philippians 4:11-13). Not all the time, but when I am in that space, it is wonderful. I want to labor to stay there.

Brennan Manning wrote, "To live in the wisdom of accepted tenderness is to accept myself and everything that happens to me as a gift that is good, and my very existence is an expression of praise and thanks to God. Life becomes the divinely written script to thanks and praise."[5] We grow. If we truly give what we can to the Lord, He will take our meager little gift and use it to begin the change in us. I believe it is this knowledge that touches me so deeply whenever I hear a version of "The Little Drummer Boy" during the Christmas season. I've no gifts to bring and so all I can do is step forward and present myself as the gift. In my shame, I am tempted to think the Lord will make a face and dismiss me: "*You're* the gift?" Instead, He smiles at me and my drum. He knows what He can do with that offering. When I give the Lord my cup, He will flood my life with an ocean of freedom.

"How significant it is that Jesus came back into the same physically wounded body. . . . Our own new nature likewise arises within the very structure of what we have been. It is not that we would be okay if we could just get away from us, and move over there somewhere else and become some other personality. . . . He called us to be us, and to become that new us with the very mess we have been, now transformed by the resurrection life of Jesus in us."[6] What once frustrated me now fascinates me with the result it produced. I was so angry with the injustice of my childhood, but since I've unloaded all kinds of stuff at the cross and waited upon my Savior to do His transforming work, I can't feel sorry for what I went through. Everyone in heaven is going to have some kind of scar, some deeper than others'. We will all be able to see the life lived because of those scars, and how efficiently the Father used what He had to work with, and it will cause us to want to throw ourselves at His feet and praise Him forever and ever.

The Bible tells me to "be transformed by the renewing of your mind. *Then*"—the emphasis is mine—"*Then* you will be able to test and approve what God's will is—his good, pleasing and perfect will" (Romans 12:2). First we must be transformed! First our minds must be renewed, after being cleansed and set right. That is a lifetime journey, listening for the direction we are to take so some other part of our mind can experience the healing flow of God's compassion.

We think we are walking toward some terrific end way up ahead, that someday we will arrive at a place of enviable maturity and wisdom if we just keep plugging along. The truth is we move forward, sometimes plodding, sometimes skipping and jumping as we go, sometimes confident and assured, other times barely able to take another step with hardly an indication we've come very far at all. This is the reason we are here. Oswald Chambers said, "What we call the process, God calls the end."[7] What we think is a process toward a final goalpost, where at some point in life we will be a blazing beacon of the renewing power of the Holy Spirit, is what the Father calls His end work. This pushing forward, this being pulled into the light, this unceasing business of transformation is His end. When He looks upon us, He sees His end results being worked out day by day. I believe we will continue this process, this end, as we enter heaven.

I believe the older brother took his father's hand and went in to join the party. I believe his hard heart was melted when his father sat and pleaded with him and told him he was loved and desired as a son. Our heavenly Father has not left us alone. He calls to those of us who were faithful, inviting us to join the celebration and rejoice with Him for those who were lost; rejoice that we have all come home to live in our Father's house.

Notes

CHAPTER 1

1. Henri Nouwen, *The Return of the Prodigal Son* (New York: Doubleday, 1992), p. 37.

CHAPTER 2

1. Henri Nouwen, *The Return of the Prodigal Son,* p. 82.
2. Jane Ryan, *Broken Spirits Lost Souls: Loving Children with Attachment and Bonding Difficulties* (Lincoln, Neb.: iUniverse, Inc., 2002), p. 33.
3. Ibid., p. 109.
4. Ibid., p. 4.
5. Web site: American Academy of Child & Adolescent Psychology, www.aacap.org/publications/factsfam/conduct.htm
6. Ibid.
7. Jane Ryan, *Broken Spirits Lost Souls,* pp. 116, 206.
8. Ibid., p. 206.

CHAPTER 3

1. Philip Yancey, *What's So Amazing About Grace?* (Grand Rapids, Mich.: Zondervan, 1997), p. 98.
2. Henri Nouwen, *The Return of the Prodigal Son,* p. 76.
3. Ibid., p.76

CHAPTER 4

1. *NIV Study Bible, New International Version* (Grand Rapids, Mich.: Zondervan, 1985), p.1570. Note on Luke 15:28.
2. Philip Yancey, *What's So Amazing About Grace?,* p. 54.

3. William L. Coleman, *The Pharisees' Guide to Total Holiness* (Bloomington, Minn.: Bethany House Publishers, 1977), p. 7.
4. Oswald Chambers, *My Utmost for His Highest* (Westwood, N.J.: Barbour and Company, Inc., 1935), p. 176.
5. John and Paula Sandford, *The Transformation of the Inner Man* (Tulsa: Victory House, 1982), p. 53.

CHAPTER 5

1. Peter Shabad, *Despair and the Return of Hope* (Northvale, N.J.: Jason Aronson, Inc., 2001), p. 82.
2. John and Paula Sandford, *The Transformation of the Inner Man*, p. 42.
3. William Coleman, *The Pharisees' Guide to Total Holiness,* p. 4.
4. Brent Curtis and John Eldredge, *The Sacred Romance* (Nashville: Thomas Nelson, 1997), p. 101.
5. Philip Yancey, *What's So Amazing About Grace?,* p. 54.
6. Ibid., p. 54.
7. John and Paula Sandford, *The Transformation of the Inner Man*, p. 41.

CHAPTER 6

1. Peter Shabad, *Despair and the Return of Hope,* p. 77.

CHAPTER 7

1. John and Paula Sandford, *The Transformation of the Inner Man*, p. 92.
2. Ibid., p. 122.
3. John and Paula Sandford, *Restoring the Christian Family* (Tulsa: Victory House, 1979), pp. 303-304.
4. John and Paula Sandford, *The Transformation of the Inner Man*, p. 108.
5. C. S. Lewis, *A Grief Observed* (San Francisco: Harper-Collins, 1961), pp. 57-58.

6. John and Paula Sandford, *The Transformation of the Inner Man*, p. 116.

CHAPTER 8

1. Henri Nouwen, *The Return of the Prodigal Son,* p. 81.
2. Brent Curtis and John Eldredge, *The Sacred Romance*, p. 50.
3. Oswald Chambers, *My Utmost for His Highest*, p. 183.
4. John Osteen, *The Divine Flow* (Houston: John Osteen Publications, 1978), p. 16.
5. Brennan Manning, *The Wisdom of Accepted Tenderness* (Denville, N.J.: Dimension Books, 1978), p. 44.
6. Helmut Thielicke, *How the World Began* (Philadelphia: Muhlenberg, 1961), p. 62.
7. Brent Curtis and John Eldredge, *The Sacred Romance*, p. 53.

CHAPTER 9

1. Henri Nouwen, *The Return of the Prodigal Son,* p. 83-84.

CHAPTER 10

1. Oswald Chambers, *My Utmost for His Highest,* p. 83.

CHAPTER 11

1. M. Scott Peck, *People of the Lie* (New York: Simon & Schuster, 1983), p. 171.

CHAPTER 12

1. Thomas Merton, *Life and Holiness* (The Abbey of Gethsemani, Inc., 1963), p. 117.
2. Oswald Chambers, *My Utmost for His Highest,* p. 68.
3. John and Paula Sandford, *Restoring the Christian Family,* p. 305.
4. Philip Yancey, *What's So Amazing About Grace?,* p. 104.
5. Ibid., p. 42.

CHAPTER 13

1. Oswald Chambers, *My Utmost for His Highest,* p. 366.
2. A. W. Tozer, *The Pursuit of God* (Harrisburg, Penn.: Christian Publications, Inc., 1948), p. 47.
3. John and Paula Sandford, *The Transformation of the Inner Man,* p. 28.
4. Henri Nouwen, *The Return of the Prodigal Son,* p. 83.
5. Brennan Manning, *The Wisdom of Accepted Tenderness,* p. 21.
6. John and Paula Sandford, *The Transformation of the Inner Man,* p. 112.
7. Oswald Chambers, *My Utmost for His Highest,* p. 210.

10716954R0

Made in the USA
Lexington, KY
15 August 2011